BEHIND
PRISON WALLS

Behind Prison Walls is dedicated to those
folks who backed me, taught me, followed me,
and tolerated me while I worked at the
McNeil Island Corrections Center and Tacoma
Pre-Release, and to all correctional staff members everywhere.

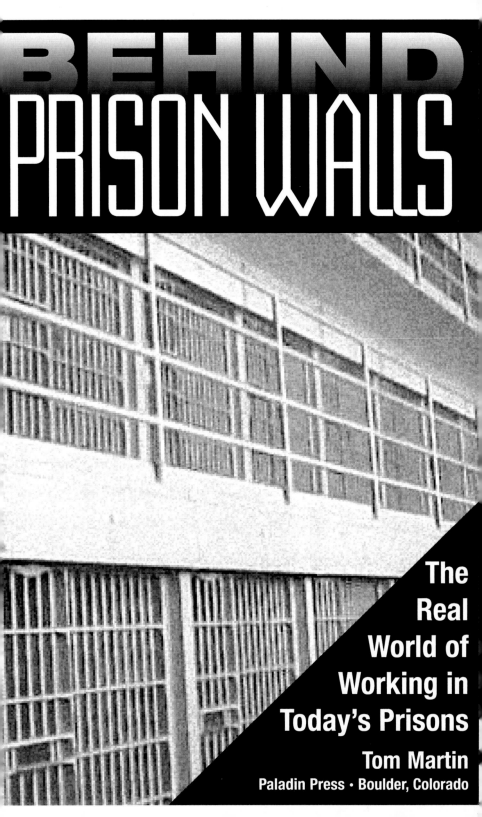

BEHIND
PRISON WALLS

The
Real
World of
Working in
Today's Prisons

Tom Martin
Paladin Press • Boulder, Colorado

Behind Prison Walls:
The Real World of Working in Today's Prisons
by Tom Martin

Copyright © 2003 by Tom Martin

ISBN 13: 978-1-58160-391-0
Printed in the United States of America

Published by Paladin Press, a division of
Paladin Enterprises, Inc.,
Gunbarrel Tech Center
7077 Winchester Circle
Boulder, Colorado 80301 USA
+1.303.443.7250

Direct inquiries and/or orders to the above address.

PALADIN, PALADIN PRESS, and the "horse head" design
are trademarks belonging to Paladin Enterprises and
registered in United States Patent and Trademark Office.

Visit our Web site at www.paladin-press.com

Table of Contents

SECTION 2: THE INMATES   45

SECTION 3: THE STRUGGLE   103

Disclaimer:
Read this First!

hile I am confident this book provides better and more detailed information on understanding and dealing with convicted felons and correctional officers then most academies and manuals, it is not to be considered an official text for people entering the field of Corrections, nor is it a professional reference for handling specific situations involving inmates or criminals. In fact, some of the techniques described should *not* be used for managing offenders. Instead, I strongly advise that correctional professionals learn the policies and procedures of their own facilities, use their chain of command appropriately, and rely on their own experience.

Staff member names that initially appear in italics are actual names of present and former correctional officers. In these cases, I am giving credit where it is due, and permission was received from each individual. In the case of inmates, no actual names are used, as it matters little to the average reader and because of privacy and confidentiality concerns.

The publisher, author, and distributors of this book disclaim any responsibility for any injury or damage to persons or property, or any misconduct or harm allegedly caused directly or indirectly, by use or misuse of any information in this book.

Behind Prison Walls is intended for entertainment purposes only.

Preface

I stumbled into Corrections on a lark. I had been an army officer, and while I still share a kinship with guys and gals who have served in the military, while there I found myself too flexible to work within a rigid structure and too inflexible to adapt to it. I was not a rule follower, and I didn't like to follow other people's approved procedures. I didn't like uniforms, hated crowds and lines, and I sure wasn't nosy, as the last thing I wanted to do was poke around someone else's stuff or find out what they were doing. With all that in mind, I filled out an application to become a corrections officer, mirthfully assuming I couldn't be more unsuited for the job.

Of course, I was hired.

Yet from the very beginning, I found work in Corrections fascinating. Within my first six months, displays of incredible courage, panic-stricken flight, biting tragedy, and natural comedy were played out before me. In my time in Corrections, I've seen young women face down fierce killers that most men feared. I've met an inmate who sacrificed his future for another. I learned of a boy who avenged his sister's death. I've spent long hours rapping with killers. I've been backed up while facing several enraged inmates, and I've had a partner bail on me and run. I've had friends hurt at work, and I've met people across the country and even across time (retirees) who did the same job and shared a kinship with them. These were rich, emotional experiences with real stakes that I would have paid to read about and learn from, yet I was paid to be there and witness them myself.

So a whim became a job, a job became a career, and a career helped change my beliefs and values and led to personal growth . . . at a price.

Introduction

orrections is a modern term for *penology*, which is the study and practice of the management and rehabilitation of criminal offenders during their incarceration. Compared to such other disciplines as government, military science, and agriculture, penology is relatively new, and "corrections" is the most recent concept in the field, following penitentiary, reformatory, and other approaches to imprisoning criminals.

Assumptions made about prisons and the treatment of inmates are embedded in our culture. Rightly or wrongly, certain prisons have become notorious throughout history. The Bastille, Devil's Island, Alcatraz, the gulags, and prison hulks represent oppression and menace rather than attempts to protect society from lawbreakers. Such places are often used as benchmarks by contemporary social critics to show how we've failed to progress, with the inmates too often elevated to martyr status.

Ironically, although seen as places of obsolescence, enforced tedium, and restraint, prisons frequently were among the most modern facilities in the United States, sporting such innovations as video surveillance, metal detectors, and even flush toilets on a large scale many years before such things were available to the general public. More importantly, heavy investment in advanced forms of social reform and psychological treatment, in both experiments and adopted programs, demonstrates a serious effort to reach a lofty goal—to return felons to society as productive, law-abiding citizens.

The people who constitute the workforce for these facilities are drawn to the field for a variety of reasons, yet few of them are prepared for working unarmed in close confines with violent offenders and the bleak, danger-

1

ous environment this collection of felons produces. Unfortunately, most of the books and magazine articles written about Corrections are just plain wrong. That is why I have written this book.

Writing about the grim, dirty reality of Corrections wasn't difficult. On a routine basis, those of us in the field witness and discuss aspects of inmate life that might stun the average person not involved in criminal justice or law enforcement. While often fascinating, little of this material is available to the public, and what is available—mainly scholarly works and official reports—is often full of jargon and steeped in officialese or so heavily distanced from reality that it is at best a superficial look at prison life. In most cases, the writers do not have enough hands-on experience within correctional facilities to provide a detailed and accurate perspective.

In a few gritty works, usually written by inmates, the reality of prison life is touched upon, but these books usually do not convey anything more than the bias of an inmate who didn't understand everything that was occurring or why things happened around him. Such authors are often too interested in vindicating themselves to provide a realistic view of the total picture.

Of course, I am biased too, and that will be evident as you read this book. To provide a quick and dirty example: Some writers and correctional "professionals" argue that it shouldn't matter to an officer whether an inmate is in prison because he assaulted someone who attacked his 12-year-old daughter, or because he is the child-murdering rapist with a rap sheet a mile long who attacked that 12-year-old. Well, it does matter, and it affects how we interact with individual inmates—sometimes subtly, sometimes blatantly. Such an attitude may not be by-the-book or even always fair, but it is a reality of Corrections that I understand and accept.

The majority of the time, correctional officers display true professionalism by treating every inmate fairly no matter what their offense. We remember that it "ain't our job to punish them," so we don't take it personally (or we usually don't).

Some portions of this book are exceptionally graphic and offensive. My desire for accuracy and the proper conveyance of atmosphere overrode sensitivity when I wrote it. Reality is harsh, and life in prison ain't no joke. In fact, no one working in Corrections can truly be unaffected by the experience. A tremendous reality of Corrections is that everyone, staff and inmate, is changed by doing time.

In Corrections, as with many other aspects of life, *perception equals reality*. Yet our perception of ourselves can often vary greatly from reality, and because of that we must be careful. Therefore, this book includes information gleaned from conversations and interviews with scores of current and former workers and inmates. I strived to provide as much reality as possible by reporting roughly commonly held views while letting the reader know when I stray from the majority opinion.

I am very aware that many officers who happen to be women might object to my using the term "female officer" and perhaps might take it as either an unnecessary distinction or, worse, a sexist approach. That, of course, isn't my intent. One of the most blazing realities, both in Corrections and in life, is that there *is* a difference between men and women. To some readers, I may be displaying a keen eye for the obvious. For many in official and politically correct circles, I'm spouting heresy by being honest. But it's simple: with many issues and events, perspectives will differ between men and women. To expose the true reality of Corrections, I have to state this up front.

Behind Prison Walls is *not* a historic record, and parts of the text required the use of literary devices rather then strict literal records. An example would be when I compiled the details of incidents that essentially occured the same across the country, year after year, and put them together in a more logical fashion. Another would be my use of inmate composites, as long as the flavor and meaning of the story weren't compromised. Finally, much of what appears in quotes as dialogue are *not* actual quotes; they represent the gist of conversations. In some cases, the specific wording wasn't recorded (writing down exactly what someone said is a bit difficult when juggling handcuffs, putting on gloves, and dealing with irate inmates), or it wasn't necessary to convey a point. In other cases, verbatim quotes were inappropriate because they might involve an inmate's real name or describe a situation too precisely, jeopardizing the safety of the offender.

Please remember, this book portrays a dark, dirty, gritty world to provide insight and entertainment, not training. There simply is no substitute for being there.

That said, a great deal about working in prisons can be learned by reading *Behind Prison Walls*. Understanding the role of correctional staff is essential to understanding the book, so the first section is about officers. This is followed by a section on the different types of felons, including revealing information on how murderers think and what female inmates are really like. Once the characters in this human drama have been established, I explain the continual struggle between the officers and the inmates and the realities of doing our job. A comprehensive glossary of correctional terms— the largest I've seen and one I compiled over many years—completes the book. Some readers may need to refer to the glossary while reading, as the language of prison salts many paragraphs, and pacing and priorities prohibit explaining some words in context.

If a reader would like to contact me to discuss any portion of the book or ask any questions, you can contact me by e-mail at grimstories@aol.com or through my publisher:

Tom Martin • c/o Paladin Press
P.O. Box 1307 • Boulder, CO 80306

I love to hear from readers.

Author's Note to Fellow Correctional Staff Members

I'd like save current and former staff members and adminstrators from trying to figure out who's who in this book in those sections where it's not spelled out. To write this book, I've contacted officers from the Pacific Northwest to the Deep South, from upstate New York to Southern California.

For anyone who sees a positive example and wishes to believe that story is about you, *it is you* as far as I'm concerned, because I'd like you to get credit if you've done something similar.

For anyone who becomes offended, believing that I'm defaming you, remember: (1) you're not that unique; there are other numb nuts as bad as you working in Corrections, and (2) you're snitching yourself off; it is likely I am referring to another officer or incident, but thanks for pointing it out.

SECTION 1

THE STAFF

7

Through the Sally Port

e stepped through the small area between two sliding doors into a long corridor. When the sliders clanged behind us, we transitioned between the free world and the inside of a prison. I studied the change in mood of the people around me. Conversations continued, but laughs now seemed forced. Smiles diminished a bit, and some grew quiet. We had entered the prison, and the *awareness* of this fact either returned or sharpened.

Five days a week, for 40 or more hours, correctional officers, sergeants, lieutenants, counselors, secretaries, nurses, doctors, and teachers are individually locked in a prison. Five days a week, for 40 or more hours, without having been convicted of crimes, we all do time.

WHAT THE F*CK?

When I was really, really new, I started off working Roving Patrol, which meant I was handed a shotgun, a revolver (Remington 870 and Ruger Security Six, for those concerned with such things), ammo, a radio, and a beat-up pickup truck and given vague instructions.

"You just drive around once in a while, but mostly park at that far corner," I was told by a guy far more interested in going home then telling a new guy anything. "Don't shoot yourself by accident."

Someone else told me that the truck was a *tower*, as if that explained everything. "Just man it like a tower."

Then I was left alone.

All I had to go on were post orders from another facility that the departing officer warned me weren't appropriate at all for my post. Post orders are the guides for the various jobs in Corrections, and one of the first things I'd been told was that I had better find them for my post the minute I got there or I'd be fried.

I drove around and occasionally parked at the one corner of the facility missing a tower. I sat there night after night, hating life, bored. I fought sleep. I examined those damn fences (actually, belts of fences) in detail. Because I was new, I didn't read, and I didn't listen to the radio. I drove around occasionally, but mostly I just sat there.

My only excitement came when someone came walking by the facility one night wearing khaki similar to what the inmates wore. I stopped the individual, keeping the shotgun in the truck (as that seemed like an overreaction) but with the revolver in its leather holster now on my belt.

"Don't you know who my father is?" demanded the teen, after stating his name.

"No," I replied, not caring.

"Well, he's going to know who you are," the kid snapped.

"Yeah, and he's going to know that you loitered by the fence at around two in the morning dressed like an inmate without any ID on you," I tossed back.

For some reason no one bothered to follow up on this incident, but if I'd followed my only available post orders—a photocopy of some other facility's posts, unsuitable for our location and very strict—*everyone* would have known who I was. I might have even made the news for a use-of-force issue that wasn't.

One day I got a radio call that I was going to be "mandatoried." This meant I had to work a mandatory overtime shift. I started my second shift inside the facility, but then, for a variety of reasons, I was sent to a small, camplike place called the Annex.

A van rushed me to some old concrete structures in the middle of some fields. A curt sergeant growled that I was late, and an officer scooped me up and directed me to a building away from the main structure. He directed me toward a door. "They're waiting," he stated and vanished.

I walked through the door. A group of a dozen or more inmates were waiting for me.

"He's here," one said. They grumbled and started yanking off shirts and grabbing belt buckles.

"What the fuck?!" I blurted. "Get over by that wall!" I snapped. The now confused inmates moved reluctantly, then quickly. I grabbed for my radio.

"What the hell is going on?" I demanded.

"You have to strip-search them before they see their visitors," replied the other officer. "Damn, how new are you?"

"Too damn new," I stated.

It was at that moment that I understood the promise that other new officers have made to themselves. I made a similar one. When I gained experience and green hires came in fresh off the streets, I'd approach them and give them any help they needed. They'd never be treated as I had been. Although there *were* many good folks there, ready and willing to mentor, at that point I didn't know who they were.

What I also didn't know was how few of the other new officers who made that pledge would last long enough to fulfill it.

MENTAL HELL-TH

The six weeks I spent cooped up in the cab of that pickup truck for eight hours a night without a radio other than the duty-issue Motorola, with no one to talk to and without reading material, got to me. Sitting alone is a very vulnerable experience; all self-doubt emerges. Coping is possible if one can focus. I couldn't focus, so my thoughts drifted.

I sat there and replayed events in my mind, running through the dialogue because I learn things better when I "hear" it. (It's similar to talking to oneself, but not too much so, I hope.) Every major and many minor mistakes I had made came to mind. It put my budding career in perspective, but unfortunately, it developed into a mild form of paranoia.

For a few days toward the end, I used another vehicle that had an AM/FM radio. I was naughty and played it. Art Bell does a late-night talk show covering truly weird topics, and he brings in people who have all sorts

---

The Wiseman

I owe the Wiseman a great deal because he helped me survive while other new officers fell by the wayside.

The Wiseman simply wanted to do an eight-hour shift with as few problems as possible. He didn't want to stir up trouble, and he worked to end situations quickly and at the lowest possible level. He continually de-escalated potential incidents using humor, giving him one of the highest rates of resolving problems that I've seen. I was new at the time I worked with him, so I didn't realize how good he was at keeping a unit quiet until after I had gained more experience. Yet his actions conveyed the wisdom of his ways to me, and I took it to heart.

Fortunately, or unfortunately, the Wiseman also had an impish side when he was restless. A significant event took place before I started working that displayed this side of his personality.

From what I understand, an inmate on an outside crew took off one night and was hiding in the bushes near his work location. The Wiseman, as was his habit, showed up early. When informed of the situation, he walked out, still holding his insulated coffee cup, and tried to locate the felon. Whether he figured out precisely where the guy was or not was incidental. He simply scanned the terrain and decided that he wasn't going to go tearing through brush or up a slope in the dark. Figuring that he probably couldn't be seen clearly either, he called out to the hidden would-be escapee, "Come on down or I'll have to let the dog go. Wolf! Wolf!"

The errant criminal ran down the hill and was put in custody without incident. But before he was led away, he asked, "Where's the dog?"

The Wiseman didn't even spill a drop of coffee.

---

of credentials. To actually hear people get into serious discussions about the Roswell UFO incident and the concept of polar shift was new and fascinating to me. I had not thought about fringe or pseudoscience stuff for years. After a while, some of it started getting to me. Odd notions—such as how *did* the coal fields and oil fields form if there wasn't polar shift—began to make sense. That realization disturbed me. I started the engine and raced to the base of the tower, desperately needing some normal conversation.

"I had to talk to someone. All that crap about aliens and scavenger technology was getting to me," I explained, calling up to the tower hoping to get into a discussion about fishing or hunting.

The officer in the tower responded: "Me too. I think the guest's basic premise is wrong. He's missing the key points, which are . . ."

I gladly departed from that position to go inside to supervise a unit, where I would only have to worry about murderers, gangbangers, arsonists, and butt pirates—individuals representing a horrible reality, but at least a *reality*.

I GET LUCKY

I was a part of D Unit, otherwise known as Dog Unit, from its establishment. Fresh from the academy (memories of which I mostly suppressed), I was eased into the duties of a unit officer because we had only a small number of inmates initially. I wasn't thrown into an existing unit with long-term, established residents who had locked in their status and power bases; rather, ours was a collection of uprooted inmates who'd not organized themselves. We filled a good part of that void and maintained most of that control as the number of inmates increased.

The staff of D Unit consisted of a good number of new officers with a salting of experienced staff. Of the experienced officers, I'd rate them above average—all of them were good (or good enough), all of them were above playing games, and all of them were secure people who knew the job and didn't feel threatened by the new officers.

Most importantly, the D Unit's dayshift sergeant was an exceptionally strong leader. The dayshift sergeant is any unit's anchor, and he can make or break the unit. D Unit's sergeant was *Lloyd Shannon*, and he didn't take any slack or give any. The man knew how to run a unit and manage inmates. I haven't met anyone worth a shit who didn't respect Shannon when he was running D Unit.

He was also old school. I remember one inmate, a disruptive, insolent fool who attempted to buck up and challenge Shannon, thinking he was a tough guy.

Shannon responded, "Any time! This blue shirt comes off easy and the stripes can go with it. I can get a *new* job," or words to that effect as he rose. Shannon had a black panther tattooed on his forearm, and he shaved his head long before it was the common thing to do, making him intimidating.

But it was the look in his eyes that caught the inmate's attention. The offender gulped, then cowered. The sergeant turned away from him in disgust, looked toward me, and said, "Get him out of here!"

Minutes later I was dropping off a memo and asked Lloyd what he would have done if the inmate took him up on the offer. The old sergeant just flashed a grin and said nothing.

It wasn't exactly PC, and it certainly wasn't what I'd been taught in the academy, but the truth is, after the incident the kid's behavior turned around. Once his bullshit bravado was gone, he had a chance to make something of himself. We never had another problem with that inmate in the year or so he was in the unit.

To me, that incident was an example of professionalism. It wasn't always about doing it in the nice, approved manner; it was about using the best technique for the moment and getting something done in a manner that made it stick.

The D Unit environment gave me enough solid training and experience that I had a good perch from which to observe other folks making errors and losing their jobs, whereas I was stopped before doing typical new guy stupid things. Ultimately, everyone of the new officers who started the unit and worked for Lloyd Shannon and wanted the rank made sergeant, including *Alex Daniels, Jason Bennett, Joe Schrum,* and myself. I can say with certainty that none of us were much different than the horde of officers who started around the same time we did. Yet the vast majority of our peers returned to the private sector by the time we made sergeant. This level of leadership wasn't matched by any other unit sergeant, although some others were spectacular as well.

Unfortunately, other sergeants were terrible, and officers assigned to work for them had little chance of making it because the leadership and example wasn't there. By watching the good and observing the bad, I learned my own style for dealing with inmates.

But all that came later. Unfortunately, for a while I was simply a new guy.

GETTING ACCEPTED

One incident can make or break a new officer. For me, it took a fight, with blood on the floor, to get accepted as a correctional officer by my senior peers.

Although I was still new and it was still a new unit, I'd been dealing with inmates regularly and developing my style. I didn't really have a need to be liked by people, and I didn't want to be buddies with criminals. I studied inmate behavior and staff techniques like a college course, all the while watching other young officers drop out as I made mistakes that were less significant than theirs.

I was enjoying the last few minutes of a shift when a call came out over the radio: "Officer needs assistance!" Being young and eager, I responded by sprinting out of my unit rather then staying where I was supposed to and securing the area. I ran into the sunlight, then burst into the relative darkness of another dimly lit unit. I didn't see any staff members, but there were dozens of agitated inmates in the dayroom, screaming encouragement to each other and defiance toward us.

This was my first response to an incident, and I was doing it wrong. I'd rushed into a darkened unit, knowing an officer was calling for help, without checking it out first. Some of the khaki-garbed criminals simply stood in the middle of the room and stared at me. I didn't see any other officers. But I didn't care. An officer needed assistance. I was doing *something*.

I went around the room looking for the officer, moving by instinct more than training, ordering the inmates to return to their rooms. The felons glared in defiance, so I started pointing to individuals.

"Lock up!"

"Go to your cell!"

"Sawyer, I got you; lock up!"

"Johnson, you're interfering!"

This technique made them scatter, and the dayroom emptied in seconds. I didn't know it, but at the same time a female officer, just as new, was on the other side of a pillar doing the same thing.

Then I noticed an open cell door, the brighter light attracting me like a moth. An inmate sprang backwards out the door, followed by two hands reaching for him. The arms were sleeved in blue—custody staff.

I ran forward, and four things happened instantly.

I wrapped my arms around the inmate and locked my hands, trapping his arms.

I realized that this was a lean, muscular inmate.

I wondered, "What the hell do I do now?"

I knew my recent academy training was worthless for this situation.

As the inmate struggled and I held on, a blue swarm exploded into the room. I released the inmate and spun just as it hit us. The Quick Response Team (QRT) and back-up in the form of reliefs from the next shift took the guy down hard. He was still struggling and fighting, so I jumped back in and grabbed a leg, or rather secured it in an unorthodox but very decisive manner. He stopped kicking with that leg, and after I barked something, his other leg stopped as well. I noticed that the female officer from the dayroom was on one of his arms, showing no hesitation and no pity.

"Good job, Tom," said one of the old-timers, who until that moment called me "Officer Martin." A few others nodded at me.

A sergeant came out of nowhere and started yelling at the newbies, "Get back to your units!" I already had hands on, so he ignored me and those of us directly involved in the dog pile. The felon's head was turning left and right, and his teeth were flashing. Someone grabbed the leg I already secured, and a sergeant blurted out, "Secure his head."

No, I thought, you do it. I wasn't *that* new.

I ignored that order as we continued cuffing him up. I helped jerk him to his feet, and I escorted the handcuffed inmate to a holding cell. As I started to leave, the inmate felt the compulsion to start yakking and explain his side of things, so I made mental notes.

Walking back, I noticed small splatters of blood on the floor leading from where I'd grabbed the inmate to the small cell reserved for containing disruptive inmates. I raised my hand to wipe sweat from my brow and saw blood on my thumb and forefinger. An exposure to bodily fluids! I knew from orientation that I was about to enter a paperwork hell, although I felt I wasn't at any kind of risk. I started wiping it off when a sergeant walked over.

"Don't you ever, ever respond without getting gloves on," he barked.

"It happened too fast."

"Learn to put your gloves on when running," he explained in a more patient tone.

I nodded.

"Otherwise, good job."

As it turned out, the officer and the sergeant who were the first responders had thrown the inmate off his cellie and out of the cell when I'd seen him. Instead of an inmate spinning away from a grab, he'd been an aggressor who'd been ejected from a fight when I grabbed him.

I saw the pugnacious prisoner several years later. He was a bit mentally unbalanced, and he'd lost a tremendous amount of weight. From what I understood, he had a nasty, terminal disease, or at least that's what he told us as we prepared to do battle with him again. The last time I saw him, he wasn't looking too good.

I always wear my gloves now.

I'd made several mistakes during that episode, but it was an important day that I still remember clearly. I'd finally been accepted by folks in the field who I respected. Strangely, this mattered more to me then graduating from college or getting commissioned as a U.S. Army officer. Not everyone is fully accepted, even after working many years in Corrections.

I'd worked hard to earn it.

2

Correctional Officers

orrectional officers, often mistakenly called prison guards, are men and women who engage in a difficult and dangerous profession not understood by members of the public. Whether working at the federal, state, or county level, correctional officers must interact with the individuals society decides must be imprisoned for acts considered to be unacceptable or shocking to the public. They maintain the safety and security of both the staff and inmates through the enforcement of policies, document and respond to observations about inmates, and occasionally implement the use of physical force to maintain order. Through these roles they protect the public.

In that lovely officialese description of the role of a correctional officer, I stressed the word *public* because it is a group that grossly misunderstands and often maligns the people who work in prisons. Many people believe we use intimidation and physical force to ensure compliance from prisoners. We do. But not all the time, and it's not the preferred method. Our techniques are much more sophisticated then mere threats and brutality.

For the most part, correctional officers are no longer knuckle-dragging goons who beat down inmates (as if most of us could!). Rather, today's officers are skilled communicators, observers, and recorders. With limited training, we must be able to make decisions based on experience, an acquired understanding of psychology, and the law. Successful officers can better predict an inmate's future actions than any highly trained shrink. They might also be called upon to use lethal force in situations where a police officer might not even draw his sidearm. On a daily basis, officers demonstrate displays of courage that few in the public could imagine.

Correctional officers do this under harsh scrutiny and threats against their life and livelihood every day, and for nominal pay. Not many people can do the job successfully. A friend of mine, a state trooper and a Marine Corps Sea Cobra pilot during Desert Storm, once told me that there was no way he'd work in Corrections. He couldn't imagine going into buildings with thousands of inmates without a firearm on hand.

Yet for those who take to the work, it can be an undeniably satisfying and fascinating career. People at parties and social events turn in rapt attention when I talk about what I do for a living. I recently enthralled an aerodynamics engineer from NASA, a surgeon, and a manager at a Silicon Valley software firm with a simple discussion on inmate manipulation.

Why wouldn't any guy want to do this job?

A NEW OFFICER'S BIGGEST THREAT

Before I began working in Corrections, I assumed that the biggest threat to a new officer might be fear of or actual violence from the criminals. I assumed that being in close confines with murderers, rapists, gangbangers, and psychos would make this the clear focus.

I was incredibly wrong.

The peril that disruptive and devious offenders present isn't the primary focus for most staff. As amazing as it sounds, that threat isn't as great as it could be. Since most officers understand that locked-up felons are dangerous (after all, many of them wish to manipulate, swindle, and violently assault prison staff), they are aware of that threat and act accordingly (with the exception of a minority who will be compromised by inmates no matter what). The nasty reality of Corrections is that most new officers wind up being more worried about their peers than the felons!

Superficially viewed, there's much merit to the assumption that the staff, not the inmates, presents a new person's biggest threat. A harsh reality of Corrections, one of many I learned from day one, is that not everyone working with me wanted me there. Some of the veteran officers aren't enthusiastic, and they see new, spirited officers as a threat. They can be more harsh to an inexperienced officer than the inmates, and they will notify supervisors immediately if a newbie screws up. They might even give erroneous information or play games with a new officer to get him or her in

---

Ducks

For some odd reason, in Corrections we call new officers "ducks." Generally, a duck is a person wearing a badge who is newer than you. Some folks are perpetual ducks because of their behavior and their inability to "get it." The more irritated a person is about being called a duck, the more likely he'll remain one; that's the way it is. Folks who don't care about the label already know they have other priorities and concerns.

trouble or to test that person—sometimes good naturedly, sometimes as a form of hazing, but as frequently, out of sheer maliciousness.

Many rookie officers (frequently called "ducks") aren't prepared for this relatively harsh treatment from their co-workers. But the fact is, because of the dangers, the job requires a rugged mind-set and emotional toughness. Officers are scrutinized and judged by tough standards, and mistakes aren't always forgiven. Part of the reason for this is because a weak officer is a threat to all. It's in the best interest of the experienced officers to retain only the most capable new hires, with some disagreement as to criteria.

Some folks simply don't belong in Corrections. They will never fit in, even with incredible support and training. It's often not due to some fault in their personality or demeanor but to what in other circles might be considered a positive trait, such as personal warmth or friendliness. A good officer isn't normally a very nice, overly compassionate person. The reality is, it takes tough people to control felons.

While it appears there is truth to the belief that fellow staff members present the biggest threat to an officer's career, this is an incomplete view. The truth is, whether an officer is new or experienced, the biggest threat to his or her career is his or her own actions and decision making. In every situation where an officer was terminated or decided to quit the field, it was because that individual made stupid mistakes; the actions and attitudes of other staff were incidental. Most likely, someone (or several people) warned the officer and attempted to steer him in the right direction. But there was nothing anyone could do if he violated certain policies or shunned tasks and aspects of the job.

Because I wanted to survive and thrive in the field, I did my best to learn how others fell by the wayside and what patterns of behavior indicated a low chance for success. I learned why they got in trouble, and I studied the events just as I'd studied for finals in college, reading related policies and informally interviewing people involved. After several years, I realized I had accumulated a tremendous amount of information—enough to compile this book.

A TYPICAL OFFICER

A typical correctional officer? There is no such thing.

In a unit, you may find a retired army sergeant major working beside a young single mom, races incidental. Their relief may include someone who lives an "alternate lifestyle," and another may be preparing for the bar exam. An officer may be related to someone in Administration and would otherwise not have a job, or he may be a worker who was downsized from another industry, or maybe she worked in another part of the department and transferred. An officer may simply be a correctional professional who wanted to get into the field, attended a vocational course to do so, and has a criminal justice degree or is working toward that goal. This type is becoming more common as the Corrections profession becomes more sophisticated.

I've worked with grandmothers, former police officers, semi-reformed hoods, and many military retirees. I've worked with college-educated communications specialists, computer-centered geeks, knuckle-dragging goons, and Nazi-cop wannabes. Some of these folks have been hard-core, and some have been easygoing. Most fall between the extremes, which is precisely where they want to be since the extremists get clipped off the ends. (Note: "hug a thug" liberals are underrepresented, for obvious reasons.)

Officer types run the gamut from enthusiastic beginners and nurturing old-timers to the opposite side: the "world owes me a living" newbie and the paycheck-drawing dinosaur with more time in uniform than the newbie's got on Earth. Some people who I really like as friends are lousy correctional officers; other individuals who I can't stand personally are incredible managers of inmates. (I'd much rather work with the latter than the former.) There is simply no way to judge from their attitudes, pasts, and motivations to get into the field who is going to be a solid officer and who is a going to be an "eight and a gate" slacker. Any of them may be as useful as green Jell-O in a serious incident, or they may be among the most courageous people I've ever met, people I'd be honored to serve beside anywhere.

Like anyone, I've met people who've worked in a wide variety of fields and gotten to know many of them really well. Without a doubt, some of the finest people I've ever known have been in Corrections. This is no surprise to people who have been there. I also must admit that some of the most repugnant individuals I've met were working in Corrections, which is a significant statement considering my exposure to convicted felons. Fortunately, the really bad ones were a scant minority.

Some old-timers have an expression: "I'd go through the door with him anytime." This is high praise, indicating they'd trust the individual enough to go into a cell extraction with them. The majority of long-term officers reach that level; many of the cowards get weeded out. So whether you love your co-workers or hate them, when help is needed, nothing else matters but a willingness to back each other up.

CARTOON OFFICERS

Most people who enter Corrections are enthusiastic, dedicated individuals who are eager to begin their jobs right. Before their first day at work, some make sure they have as many resources related to Corrections and law enforcement as possible, and they buy everything they think will help them succeed. Gradually, most find out what they really need in order to do the job and bring just that, but there are exceptions.

"RoboCops" are those individuals who think they'll be transformed from the socially awkward, uptight individuals they are to crime-fighting studs because they get to wear a uniform and a badge. In an earlier generation, they were mockingly called "Super Cops."

Generally, RoboCops are either much leaner or heavier than average, with very few in the middle. They are likely to wear mirrored shades (if they aren't wearing horned-rim glasses) and have carefully combed hair and overly attended beards and mustaches. These so-called professionals always seem to wear the uniform wrong, either never ironing it or overdoing it by putting creases where they don't belong and spending more time polishing their shoes then walking in them. Almost without fail, these guys never follow policy, don't attempt to learn it, and never listen to the sound advice of helpful staff members.

RoboCops are the most likely to be sporting what I call a BUB, or Batman Utility Belt. A BUB will have every police accessory known to man or Gall's (a major police outfitter)—belt keepers, glove pouches, cuff cases, key fobs, waterproof notebook pouches, radio holders, flashlight holders, dangling coffee cup, search mirror pouches, glove pouches, and a pouch for personal protective equipment (PPE). One officer I knew even had a special pouch for his ramen bowl! If they can manage to sneak them in, RoboCops might even have equipment they shouldn't have inside a correctional facility, such as a personal knife and pepper spray. They give the impression they are primed and ready to fight crime . . . or go camping.

Most of the underlying BUB belts are made of Cordura or jet-black basket-weave leather, without a hint of dust or a single scuff. All of the draping items match the belt, which isn't necessary since there is so much crap there that you can't see the damn belt! As they begin their shift, RoboCops make a solemn ceremony of assembling these masterpieces, putting on war faces as they reach about and affix everything to their trouser belts. The transformation is completed by a manly nod.

Too frequently, RoboCops either carry things they'll never need or lack exactly what they do need. One time, another officer bet me that a newbie would have three obscure items on his belt, and I lost when the guy pulled out stuff I didn't know *existed*. The same guy couldn't produce a damn pen—the most essential piece of officer equipment—but he had two types of flashlights, a penlight, search mirrors (one with and one without a handle), glove pouches, two cuff cases (although he was issued only one set of cuffs), and a custom holster for his radio, even though they were provided as standard issue.

That clown's performance notwithstanding, most RoboCops always have writing implements because they are quick to write up everything. With smug, tightlipped expressions on their faces, they whip out their pens from their hidden pocket protectors faster than quick-draw artists in the old West and jot down an inmate's name and number on their all-weather, combat paper, U.S. Cavalry mail-ordered, spiral-bound field pads. The snippiest ones "keep book" on staff activities as well.

My favorite moment involving Batman Utility Belts involved a guy who, while not exactly a cop wannabe, had the misfortune of providing an excellent example for this book. He had caught the belt bug and gone to the police outfitters with a credit card during those vulnerable first months on the job. We were chatting when a body alarm went off. The proud BUB wearer sprung up to respond—or attempted to as he got snagged by the armrests of his chair, which neatly entangled the crap on his belt. He sprang back, arms flailing, then rocked forward and tried to run bent over with the chair stuck to his butt! I almost fell down the stairs laughing as I ran to the emergency.

RoboCops love to posture. I use to snicker as I'd see one pose on some perch, looking down at inmates, his mirrored shades worn even on cloudy days or while inside the unit. I'd try to warn the guy that the inmates deepened their voices and acted tougher around him to provide him with more of a rugged-appearing environment, but he never caught on to my meaning.

The inmates almost always discount such an officer, except when they figure out exactly how to play the guy, which they commence as quickly as possible because they know the shelf-life of a cop wannabe is very short. They assume, perhaps correctly, that the overuse of police paraphernalia is compensation for fear or feelings of inadequacy, and the inmates are eager to exploit those traits before the duck moves on.

Some officers who wear all the crap are still good and professional at what they do. In their case, it's not a crutch or a shield but rather a matter of careful selection through experience. On the other hand, most RoboCops and their Batman Utility Belts don't make it in Corrections. They are missing something, but it's not a belt accessory. They generally end up back at their jobs as security guards, where the professionals there find them just as odd as we do. Fortunately it's a more solitary job, and the RoboCops do better there.

In contrast to the wannabe's obsession for accouterments, most experienced staff members simply toss their keys in their front pockets, shove their cuffs and radios in their butt pockets, and drive on.

Oh, and they can find their pens.

PROGRESSIVE STUPIDITY

In the field of Corrections, there are a select few who demonstrate what I call "progressive stupidity." Those afflicted with it are fast movers who become proportionately more stupid the higher they climb up the ladder, forgetting a tremendous amount of lessons that they should have learned at lower levels as they blitz to executive status.

As a hypothetical example, Officer Grundy—known for being a poor manager of inmates but otherwise unremarkable except for his sloth—suddenly becomes Sergeant Grundy, to the chagrin but not the surprise of experienced staff. In his new position of authority, he corrects an officer while that officer is doing the right thing. It becomes apparent that Grundy either didn't know his job in the first place or had forgotten what he was supposed to do. But Sergeant Grundy isn't moved back to being an officer; he gets promoted. ("Fuck up, move up," isn't limited to the military.) Now he is directing sergeants and new officers. As such, he's influencing new hires who don't know he was a messed-up officer and worthless sergeant, and they follow his example. It seems as if some brand-spanking new, brassy young female officer will always quote him, and we bite our tongues because we don't want to shoot down her faith in his leadership, knowing that if she can't interpret Grundy, she's got no chance figuring inmates.

As a former sergeant, Grundy is aware of the requirements for scheduling custody staff, or at least he should be. But he's either done another brain dump and forgot the requirements of policy, common sense, and the collective bargaining agreement, or he's never learned them. He forgets about things like relief factors, and some poor shift lieutenant—who, incidentally, remembers Grundy as a dicked-up officer—must now unscrew the mess.

That thoroughly jaded LT will tell any cagey sergeant to watch Grundy because he's going to be moving up the chain of command. Whatever got him promoted obviously didn't have to do with his knowledge and job skills, and he can't be burnt because someone risked their credibility getting the numbnuts to his current level.

Hot Mike

When the button on the mike of a Motorola radio is pressed accidentally, the person wearing the radio doesn't know that he or she is transmitting, but the entire conversation goes out and everyone else receives it. We call it a "hot mike." Someone almost always begins calling "hot mike."

This obviously can be embarrassing, as a whole lot of conversations shouldn't be broadcasted across a facility. In fact, after years of practice covering their asses, one of the common habits of experienced staff members who are discussing something they shouldn't is to shut down their radios for a few seconds just in case. I've discussed things with fellow correctional officers away from work and, although off duty and out of uniform, at times we both will reach down to switch off a radio that isn't there. Communicatively, it means that what is about to be said is juicy, a nonverbal explanation point.

One day while walking out from our shift, a sergeant who wasn't our regular shift sergeant complained that some guy had keyed his mike and broadcast a conversation all night. At that time we had a more primitive radio system, so there wasn't a ready way to tell who was keying the mike. The sergeant was trying to figure out who it was, and she wasn't known for being subtle.

I had been working with the Wiseman when the incident occurred, and we exchanged glances. A mike was keyed and we hadn't heard crap all night. Uh oh—could be us!

As usual, the Wiseman had a slick way of clearing us.

"You say someone was keying their radio and they talked all night?" he asked.

"That's right," the sarge said.

"Were they talking bad about you?"

"No," responded the sergeant, her head shaking.

"Then it couldn't have been us," the Wiseman said, turning to me and grinning.

Grundy is now a big-time decision maker, and it's his policies and ideas that will leave officers cursing, scratching their heads, or shrugging and starting to check the want ads. Fortunately, if we wait long enough, Grundy will eventually reach a position lofty enough that he's totally out of touch, and the problem will be solved. Also fortunately, Grundy types are in the minority.

HARD-CORE REALITIES CONCERNING STAFF

While the pool of officers is full of a wide variety of people, and the "desired traits" vary from facility and facility, there are certain attitudes and philosophies about Corrections that are common no matter where you work. This is the sort of stuff that human resources never tells the new hires.

Not Everyone Should Be in Corrections

Although controversial, it is a fact that not everyone can be trained to be an effective Correctional officer. Mother Teresa would have made a lousy officer (too nice); same with the Marquis de Sade (too nasty). If she whips out her checkbook every time she turns on the television and hears about some skinny kid being exploited, we don't need her—she is probably *too* compassionate for the job. If someone else utterly doesn't care about other people, or if his views of right and wrong are so strong that he feels compelled to act a certain way when he interacts with a heinous person, that person won't fit in either.

Many Correctional Officers Have Strong Personalities.

Some people view aggression, suspicion, and directness as character flaws. For correctional workers, these are necessary traits.

Really nice, friendly folks who politely wait their turn don't make it in this profession. In Corrections, we have a name for the kind-hearted and trusting—*victim*. Inmates, on the other hand, love them.

Correctional Staff Eat their Young

People drawn toward Corrections are in many ways more aggressive than the average citizen. They expect new officers to be hardened to harsh comments and sharp glances. Prisons are damn serious places, and individuals perceived as being threats to security because of incompetence, inattention, or softness receive little sympathy. Other officers are so eager to get rid of these weak links that they actively work toward that end, while the majority simply let them be themselves and work their own way out of a job—hence the expression, "We eat our young."

Officers Turn On Each Other

One grim and interesting dynamic of correctional staff is that in the absence of problems with inmates, we turn on each other. The divisiveness manifests itself in various forms, ranging from good-natured ribbing to outright hostility and, rarely, meetings in the parking lot. It's not all negative, and some of it is healthy. We may see conflict between the dinosaurs and the young inexperienced but hard-charging know-it-alls who want to take over, or it may be Custody vs. Admin, union vs. non union, unit vs. unit, individual vs. individual, or the most common, shift vs. shift. It just happens. It's a result of having many aggressive people working together.

Correctional Officers Say It Like It Is

Officers have no hesitation in calling it like they see it, sometimes loudly and repeatedly. Most of them are firm on their views, and many don't give a shit about what others think of them.

This is to be expected. Anyone who, as a part of their job description, must tell a mass murderer to go clean the toilets or who has to break up a power walk by a dozen gang members in the yard has little actual concern for the feelings of rookie officers or fear of the admin folks. The rougher the experiences of a correctional staff member, the more willing he or she is to buck up and stand up for him or herself.

No Matter How Good You Are, Someone Will Second-Guess You

Another nasty aspect of Corrections is that we continually second-guess each other. Perhaps it's an extension of our nature to enter into conflict, but more likely it is because Corrections work is complex, individual experiences vary, and our focuses differ.

I've had the bittersweet satisfaction of seeing a few individuals who attempted to undermine me fail miserably in similar situations. I don't want to see anyone fail, but vindication is sweet. I don't like this aspect of the job, but it exists, perhaps more heavily in Corrections than in other fields.

Monkey Fuckers

Throughout my time in Corrections, I witnessed individuals who defied all the odds by remaining employed. Some officers and other staff members couldn't do their jobs if their lives depended on it, yet they continued to draw pay, while others, far more competent, fell by the wayside. The bad ones included officers who intentionally messed with inmates in areas they shouldn't, such as medication, mail, food, and documentation. Bad counselors ignored inmate requests that fell within reason or left things hanging so that an offender wasn't able to see his or her family. Correcting the effects of incompetent and mean-spirited staff members is a huge part of everyone else's work.

I mentioned this to a peer, and she told me that I was blaming the wrong people.

"You need to be mad at the monkey fuckers," she stated.

I looked at her quizzically.

"Think about it. For someone to get away with what he does, he has to have a picture of someone important fucking a monkey. It's the only kind of leverage that would allow him to do what he does."

That settled it.

Correctional Officers Follow the
Convict's Code Better Than Inmates Do

Most people are aware of the semi-mythical Convict Code, shaped by inmates in the nineteenth and early twentieth centuries and made famous by classic James Cagney movies. Honor among thieves. Settle things man to man. Don't create problems and bring down heat from those above you. Do your own time. And the most important, don't snitch. All of these are expected behaviors of an experienced, stand-up inmate, a con.

Today, as the number of true cons diminish, the Code is followed less and less by the general inmate population. Ironically, it's the officers who are more likely to live by these rules nowadays. Solid officers prefer to settle things among themselves and not involve sergeants or other higher-ups, and they don't like shit stirrers.

Some Officers Become as Dirty as the Inmates

A new officer may be utterly heroic and willing to "get your back" (back you up), or he may be too lazy and stupid to get out of his chair or answer the phone. He may be a balanced, mature individual with a sense of humor and a willingness and ability to get along with his co-workers, or he may get off on angering inmates and leaving other officers to straighten it out. The worst officers become dirty and engage in illegal dealings with inmates. Bad female officers can take it a step further by engaging in sexual activities with inmates, thus eroding the credibility of female staff members everywhere. What's especially sad is that both the male and female in these examples might do these things over the duration of their careers.

Couples That Aren't

A good example of how rumors start and get out of hand occurs with relationships between male and female officers. Friendships are too often seen as intimate relationships, and because perception equals reality, it's treated that way by others (although I must state that this particular dynamic is reinforced by the fact that it happens often enough to make it a bona fide assumption in some cases).

A partner and I once observed that if a male and a female are working regularly together in a unit and it's within the realm of possibility that they could be a couple—i.e., he's got at least a vague awareness of soap and doesn't give everyone the creeps, and she's smiled at least once and doesn't devote her life to her 96 cats—then in many people's eyes they're going to be considered a couple, marital status of either party incidental. If, at the end of the shift, they walk out separately, then they are trying to cover up the relationship. If they walk out together silently or talking quietly, it's an intense relationship. If they walk out and she laughs at something he says, it's definitely on. Heaven help the female officer who carpools with a male staff member!

For a while I had a female partner who, for various reasons, didn't exactly fit the mold (in the eyes of the cheap seaters) of being a potential partner-partner with me. But I learned you can't win when a new female partner told me that she'd been warned by others that, because of the way my previous partner and I acted toward each other, I didn't like working with women! Then, because I got along with my new partner, well, another rumor started . . . .

The Dirtier the Rumor, the More Ready Folks are to Believe It

Not every person working in Corrections has an accurate sense of other people's behaviors and motives, and while some are naturally savvy through experience or classes in psychology and sociology, many don't have finely developed intuition for these things. As a result, many in the field readily believe whatever dirty rumors and gossip they hear. It just doesn't take much for a male officer to be identified a dog or a female officer to be slapped with a slut label. Furthermore, the gossipmongers will vehemently forward the nastiest of rumors with the flimsiest of evidence, although some of these same individuals frequently will defend an inmate who is obviously engaged in some illegal or improper activity.

Nothing Else Matters When a Body Alarm Goes Off

Unless it's a very odd facility, when any officer needs assistance, all the staff friction goes out the window. It's Us vs. Them, with Them being the inmates. When help is needed, it's a great feeling to see the swarm of blue, brown, or gray shirts appearing. It's then that you realize you are part of a team.

3

Forging a Team

hen I first started working in a prison, I disliked a number of the people who shared the same uniform. From day one, minute one, I was scrutinized by the experienced officers, perhaps more harshly than by the sergeants and even by the criminals. They asked questions that I knew were tests, and they acted as if I had to prove myself to them.

I kept my mouth shut for the first six months, which coincidentally was the duration of my trial service. I didn't mind hard work, and I wasn't scared of the inmates. I just kept plugging at it until one day I was one of them, a Corrections officer, accepted by those who mattered, disliked by the ones good officers wanted to be disliked by, and treated with respect by the sergeants and inmates.

I realized this transformation had taken place when they stopped looking at me like a newbie, then started talking about the newbies *with* me. Soon, I was being asked to train the newbies. Eventually I was supervising them, then directing the old-timers as I filled sergeant slots.

Not every officer goes through this transformation from duck to team member. Some don't last long enough. The fortunate ones wind up with peers and supervisors who are professionally mature and want to ensure that the newbie is a team player from the get-go. The ones who do make it have survived some of the institutional pitfalls of the Corrections field. Two of the biggest are best described as the "snake pit" and the "wolf pack."

THE SNAKE PIT

I liked Officer Gray. A young black male my age, we were becoming good friends because he was about as new as I was and had a great sense of humor about everything. He also came into the field fresh from serving in the army. We compared our observations three nights a week.

One day, Gray called me up, concern in his voice. He was in big trouble—he'd been caught sleeping. I had to ask how a former soldier could make the mistake of sleeping on duty.

"It was a trick bag. I was set up," he complained bitterly.

Gray continued: "Out here [in his area], I always see the other officer sleeping in the office. He even asked me to take over his duties once when he was really wiped out, so I did it."

"Today, I was burned. I had that OT [overtime], I get home, and Victoria starts on me on how I ain't making enough in this job, how I'm gone too much, and this and that. Ain't no sleeping with her going on. My partner tells me it's okay if I get some shut-eye and he'd cover for me, and that it's okay with the sarge cuz he did it as an officer too.

"I hold out until 3 o'clock count, then I have to take fifteen. I tell my partner and he says he'll cover. I get in the office, shut the door, and I'm out like a light. Ten minutes later, the light's on, someone wakes me up, and the sergeant is staring at me with this angry look. The LT [lieutenant] has already gotten a call on me. My partner is behind the sergeant. I can see a grin on his face, and the mutha is trying not to laugh."

We lost Officer Gray in a few weeks after he made a second major mistake, again listening to another experienced staff member and going against his better judgment. He'd fallen victim to the snake pit, where new officers are cast amid a seething mass of experienced staff members, some of whom we'd been warned might be more dangerous to our careers then inmates were to our lives. Gray learned the hard way that it was true.

THE WOLF PACK

"They ain't ever going to get rid of me, but they might get rid of you," grinned a boyish officer in his early thirties one day when we had a discussion about Corrections. "You see, I'm an Omega. You're an Alpha, risen from the pack because you're a sergeant and an army-trained leader type. All them Betas and the whole of the pack can replace you, but they don't want to be the targets yet. No one wants my spot. I gotta do something utterly horrendous to be cut."

I looked at Larry with confusion. He was one of my officers when I was a new sergeant, and I knew he was an intelligent, observant person, although he frequently got into trouble. When he had the glint in his eyes, I listened.

"Officers and sergeants belong to a wolf pack," he continued. "We eat our young when they are weak, and we shun and drive out the members of the pack who don't fit and don't have a role. It's cruel but necessary for our survival in a hostile environment."

I thought about it and realized Larry was right—the wolf pack analogy aptly described the internal dynamics of the correctional staff. Just like a wolf pack, survival of the group is essential; individuals are less important. Like a wolf pack, the new folks in Corrections, the pups, aren't coddled. They are expected to become full-fledged contributing members as soon as possible. Flawed individuals who might weaken the pack aren't tolerated. Those who don't make the cut are quickly identified and shunned because it's too dangerous to have weak links jeopardizing everyone else. Situations change quickly and sometimes violently in prison, so new officers are expected to adapt.

Such harsh treatment is not just reserved for newbies. What happens to any officer or sergeant who is unable to continue doing his or her job (being unable to respond to an assistance call, primarily) is almost chillingly callous.

"What good is he?" the others ask.

Even good friends dip their heads reluctantly and silently in agreement. I am sorry to admit that I've done it as well.

Like a real wolf pack, members of the correctional pack have specific roles. Whether officers or sergeants, Alphas are dominant, and their role puts them in more jeopardy more often than the others because they face constant challenges from the pack as well as from external threats (Administration, lawyers, etc.). Betas are strong officers who are the true strength of Corrections. They are ready to lead but often don't feel the need unless it is necessary. Most of the rest of the pack have various levels of competence and commitment, but they are still a part of it.

On the tail end of the spectrum is the butt of all jokes and common scapegoat, the Omega, an established officer who adheres to the minimum for the group's acceptance and revels in the role. Omegas catch hell from the pack, play the clown, and get the shit jobs, yet they are strong enough that they aren't culled like the weak ones. They can be seen as rebels in that they define the limits, but in a strange way they can also be seen as leaders because they take big risks and go against convention. The passing of an Alpha might be stunning, but he or she gets replaced quickly. The passing of an Omega is mourned because no one wants to take that role.

Like a wolf pack, the correctional staff fights among itself, sometimes viciously. But when there is an outside threat, such as an inmate attack on a staff member, the full fury of the pack moves into collective, coordinated action. Watching staff members slip from the different units and move down the corridors prior to becoming a swarm is akin to seeing wolves moving rapidly through the forest moments before pouncing upon prey. Correctional staff have a more measured response, but watching them respond as a pack to an outside threat is impressive. Oftentimes, it is the first indication to a new officer that beneath all the petty bullshit, a group of correctional officers is a tight team.

THE TEAM

A new officer may wonder if the job is worth putting up with such things as the snake pit and wolf pack mentalities of the staff on top of the stress of dealing with manipulative, dangerous inmates. But if an officer survives the initial trial period, he or she will experience something new when an incident develops and an officer needs assistance. When a summons for help goes out, a blue (or brown, or gray) swarm appears. Dislike, conflict, and petty game playing vanishes when everyone races to help one of ours against one or more of them, and it's a damn good feeling and a prideful moment when you experience it. It's a damn near indescribable feeling when you're the one waiting for the assistance.

To fully understand what I'm talking about, remember that correctional staff are working with murderers, rapists, gangbangers, and every heinous type of individual imaginable, outnumbering the staff not by five or ten to one but potentially hundreds to one in some locations. In the facility, an officer usually has only a radio and a set of cuffs on hand during the initial response. Yet fellow officers will race to help one another even though they might find armed inmates or even a full-blown riot in progress. There's a chance they might be shanked, punked, doused with flammables, or beaten to death, but they come running into an unknown situation to do their duty

The Gang

"You fucking officers ain't nothing but a gang!" the inmate spouted, talking boldly as he vented. "You're like us, only you got badges instead of rags, and you got the law when all we got is the street."

"How are officers and sergeants like gang members?" I asked inmate Johnson patiently, because I was interested in his model for describing custody staff.

"We wear colors, you wear colors," he replied. "Someone fucks with one of you, they gotta deal with every one of you, and if someone hurts one of you or disses [disrespects] one of your women, one of the white ones that's everybody's cutie, oh Lordie, it's over for that poor brother cuz it don't matter—white, black, Hispanic—it's on from the blue shirts. You fight with each other, I see that, but as a gang, you take us on and you take on the super and those administrators."

I fought the urge to nod in agreement. He was making his point.

"Name one thing that makes you officers different then gang members," he challenged.

"We get paid to belong," piped in my partner, who I thought was ignoring the conversation. The other inmates in the area laughed, and Johnson chuckled and gave the hands up, "I surrender" sign as he walked away.

From an inmate perspective, the custody staff is pretty much a gang, considering the basest definition of the term and leaving out the illegal activities. This reality was epitomized by an officer's response to a veiled threat from an inmate that I heard early on:

"Any ten of us can take any one of you."

and help one of their own. When the right site supervisor is on hand and decisively takes charge, the uniformed staff acts as crisply and efficiently as a Marine Corps infantry squad. It's a great thing to see, a better thing to participate in, a fantastic thing when you're the one who needed the help, and the ultimate experience of teamwork and professionalism if you happen to be the one directing the activity.

So like many who make it through the initial trial period, my perception of the group changed as I developed as an officer. From my view that I'd fallen amid a nest of vipers who could teach junior army officers a few things about back biting and sniping at one another, I eventually realized I had become a part of a tight team that I could trust with my life. Each perspective was accurate based on my understanding of the job, the environment, and my coworkers at the time.

4

Courage

One of the aspects of humanity I like to observe and learn about is courage. I enjoy having my fears tested, and I've witnessed displays of courage and, as importantly, utter cowardice. In Corrections, I was given extraordinary opportunities to study courage that I didn't even get in the military.

It takes courage to walk up to a group of inmates from a different ethnic and cultural group who are acting up. Telling a convicted murderer that he hasn't done a job right and he better go back and clean the shitters isn't a pucker factor moment, but it is a gut check for anyone with intelligence. Suiting up to take down a deranged, shank-armed inmate who proudly proclaims that he's infected with AIDS as he spits blood takes a bit of guts. Rushing to assist another officer when the prison is gripped in tension takes guts too. When the situation gets tense and when the expressions of concern cover the faces of the officers and sergeants around you, it's scary . . . but it's exhilarating.

For men and women in "big prison," the threat of a riot is always there. It's in the back of our minds. We sometimes joke about it. We fear it. We prefer to use a word like "disturbance" rather then the "r" word, the same way some religious people fear saying "the Devil."

Getting beaten or stabbed are serious fears, but the notion of being taken hostage and gang-raped by inmates is probably any man's biggest fear. We know it has happened. I can't cite the source, but I'd once heard that among a group of officers taken in one riot, the survivors had an incredible suicide rate because of the things they'd experienced while in the custody of the inmates. As a female officer once told me, women have a better chance of dealing with this scenario because they face the threat of rape (or at least the idea of it) on a regular basis; many in fact have been raped, but the vast majority of guys are totally unprepared for dealing with it.

But riots aren't the normal reality of Corrections, so displays of courage are usually limited to decisions and actions made on the spot, often in seconds. Solid decisions with good results done on a routine basis are too often overlooked, and officers who do heroic things often minimize what they've done because they know others would have done the same. Acts of cowardice cannot be retracted, and some endure years of regret over a decision or response, perhaps for the rest of their lives. At times, heroic acts are seen as stupidity; at other times, stupidity is seen as heroic. Sometimes it's simply easier to show guts no matter what common sense dictates.

One common false belief that many people have is "you don't know what you're going to do until the event actually happens." I've heard that utter nonsense for years in the military and in Corrections and realized that people who espouse that belief don't know what *they* are going to do when it happens to *them*. Their mind-set almost ensures that they will freeze up or panic precisely because they don't know what they are going to do. They are also among the quickest to second-guess others who handled the actual situation.

Honest officers tell their partners at what point they'll bolt and run. Under certain really, really bad circumstances, I am going to shit my pants and run like mad. After frantic panic, perhaps I'll cower until I get dragged down by inmates. Other situations might call for me to stand my ground—like an idiot—*and die*. In others, I'll calmly accept what's going to happen—like an idiot—*and die*. In most others I am simply going to do my job and hope to resolve the situation because another reality of Corrections is that we get paid for *what can happen to us*, not for what we do.

When an officer has training and experience and, more importantly, has anticipated what is going to occur and makes up his mind to do what is right, he will react correctly. With experience and the proper mind-set, he can make on-the-spot decisions for totally new situations and whip out solutions as if they were old techniques.

A ROUTINE EXAMPLE OF HEROISM

It was the first day in the unit for Officer Meadows, and I was her partner. She had not felt well the previous day, but being new she didn't want to call in sick. I was at a peak in my training, and I was eager to teach new people the various aspects of the job. Being given a brand new officer who was willing to learn was a bonus, and Officer Meadows was instantly likable. She had a winning smile and seemed to remind people of someone else they remembered favorably. It promised to be another easy night of work.

During the shift, I told her about the dangerous inmates in the unit. Normally we'd call inmates with the same last name by their last name and their first initial; for example, Smith, A. and Smith, R. We had one exception. I pointed out an inmate called "Murderer" Johnson to differentiate him from the other Johnsons, because that was what he was and that was how he carried himself. This distinction provided ample warning when dealing with a very angry, very powerfully built man.

Murderer Johnson was a militant Muslim. Many Muslim inmates were difficult to manage because the strict cultural requirements for such a lifestyle were new to them, and as with any group, new converts were often the most vehement of adherents. In this case, Murderer Johnson had decided that "the white woman was the Devil," and he'd be doing his part to eliminate that scourge. I told Officer Meadows that and saw it register on her now unsmiling face and larger brown eyes. Someone she didn't know and had done nothing to truly hated her just for being her. It was a stark realization for the newbie officer. Still, after giving some more pointers and warnings, I figured we would settle into a routine shift.

I figured wrong.

A group of gangbangers were attempting to take over the dayroom, challenging us by being rambunctious and noisy. They laughed too loud and too frequently, with more bitterness then mirth, and they exchanged glances with each other and glared at us, the open defiance burning in their eyes.

There were three of them, all "gangstas." I first gave them a pointed look, which didn't check them. Then I warned them verbally. They continued. The time to break them up came shortly afterward. All of the inmates in the dayroom except the three offenders grew quieter as I rose from my desk and turned toward my partner. For some reason, perhaps anticipating interesting viewing, an unusually high number of offenders lingered in the dayroom after eating. More than a hundred pairs eyes fell upon us, waiting for a confrontation.

"I'm going to send them to their rooms. Watch my back," I told Meadows. She nodded, not taking her eyes off of them.

"Baker, Green, Washington, I gave you a previous warning. Lock up." They glared at me and rose as one. They quickly stepped around the table and formed before me, arguing. I faced the three young, athletic black men in my "ready stance" (ready to get my ass kicked, I'd sometimes joke) as per procedure, realizing how little good reason would work with them and how utterly useless most academy training was when it came to handling situations like this.

"This isn't a discussion. I gave a previous warning," I stated. "I'll talk to one of you, but the others will lock up now." This technique normally worked well, allowing me to quickly identify the leader and isolate him.

The ringleader, Baker, stepped forward. I moved a few steps to one side to get him to follow me out of earshot of the others. Using standard verbal techniques, I got him to realize that he had nothing to gain from continuing and nothing to lose by backing down because he'd already "bucked up" (stood up for himself). He started to nod at what I was saying. The others merely waited on his lead. He gestured toward his room, and I felt a hint of relief.

Then it happened.

A rich, rugged voice called out from across the room.

"I'm a man. No way he could get me to lock up like that!"

I had no idea who called out, but the response was instant. The three inmates went from compliance to open defiance and confrontation in seconds. I could see it and feel it as they turned on me and advanced. For the first time since working in Corrections, I felt like I was about to get my ass whooped. I reached down and grabbed the mike that hung off my belt, ready to call for help. This gesture was more potent than any words I could have said in that moment. Besides, I figured that squeezing the mike and calling for help might be the last talking with a full set of teeth I'd be doing for a while.

Writing my own well-being off, my concern shifted from the threat immediately before me to remembering that my partner was new and she might get hurt as well. The chilling thought that maybe I could have done something different crossed my mind, but no, I was following procedure that had worked dozens of times before. I glanced back to check on my partner, hoping to see at the officer's station where I'd left her, grabbing for the phone.

She wasn't. Instead, she had situated herself closely between my back and Murderer Johnson. He was agitated and confrontational, trying to distract her and using proximity and posture in an attempt to intimidate her. I figured he had 80 pounds of muscle, 7 inches of height, 15 years of meanness, and a deep-seated resentment on Meadows. She didn't falter. She was persuading him to become uninvolved, standing her ground and speaking clearly just as a hardened, experienced officer might. At that volatile moment, Meadows was worth more to me than a Quick Response Team *because what she did worked!* Satisfied with her responses, Murderer Johnson moved on.

With renewed resolve, I continued directing the trio of young inmates until they broke and moved back to their rooms. Perhaps they'd been emboldened by Murderer Johnson's moving up on my rear, or they'd been caught up in something they didn't really want to do and decided to back off as Johnson did. Whatever the reason, they quit. Speaking in front of all the inmates in the dayroom, I then challenged the instigator by telling him to identify himself. He didn't, which I am sure meant his credibility was eroded, the impact of his words lost. The inmates quickly turned their attention back to whatever they'd been doing before the incident erupted.

The three inmates would be "unit teamed," or dealt with later by counselors, a custody unit supervisor, and the sergeant. I was completely informed about it and satisfied with the outcome, but basically we had had a non-incident, just an exchange.

Interestingly, at first Meadows didn't absorb the full danger of the situation. She'd simply reacted to what she saw as an escalating situation. I later asked her if she'd been afraid when she confronted a man who wanted to kill people like her.

"Very," Meadows replied.

"Why did you do it?" I had to ask.

"It's my job. I love my children, and this is how I plan on supporting them."

She didn't do it for me. She didn't do it to gain credibility. She did it for her children.

Incidents like this happen everyday in prisons. Most of us don't even think of it in special terms. We are just doing our jobs, and such actions are simply expected. Therefore, almost no one appreciates the courage shown daily by officers like Meadows. But I do, and it was a beautiful thing to see.

COWARDICE THAT WORKED

Perhaps that incident made an impression on me because of a previous situation where a very different level of courage was displayed. This event occurred shortly before my stand with Officer Meadows, and it involved a co-worker I'll call Officer Hideaway.

Hideaway had great instincts when it came to gauging inmate behavior, and normally that's an incredible asset to have in a partner. However, in this incident her intuition worked against her and for me when she read a situation and reacted.

Hideaway and I were sitting at the officers' station when a ding (prison slang for a mentally ill offender) approached the desk. In prison for several months, he wanted to have extended family visits (conjugal visits, or, in the parlance of a very crude inmate, time in the "fuck trailer"). But he had a problem: he'd come into the system under an alias, and his marriage license was in his real name. He'd written to his counselor three times over the weekend, and of course his three notes were in the distribution box in the counselor's empty office. So he wanted me to fix the problem. Now.

He became more and more agitated and started leaning across the desk. His fists were tightly balled and his eyes were wild. I got out of my chair and figured we'd be meeting as we crossed over the desk, because I had a partner to protect and he wasn't going to back off. Still, *high potential for tremendous pain* came to my mind.

I heard a click behind me. The inmate stared wide-eyed over my shoulder, then smiled, then started laughing. He started laughing so hard that he doubled over.

"Where your back-up?" he asked.

I backed off a bit, then angled my head. The bathroom door was closed. The phone was mounted on the wall beside it, the long cord swaying back and forth. I might have imagined the little dust swirls, but they may as well have been there.

I listened. I didn't hear water running, a locker being opened, or a bag being shuffled through. The felon was still laughing.

"Man, I am sorry, but I can't be mad now," he exclaimed, walking back to his room. I later found out that he began packing up his property, anticipating being sent to seg for his outburst. His cellie reported that the guy said, "Seeing that look on that cop's face and seeing her run was worth going to the hole."

I stood by the desk, about to call the LT for his decision, when the door opened slowly and a head popped out and looked around. I still didn't hear the water running from the toilet being flushed. Officer Hideaway turned toward me with a practiced quizzical look.

"Oh, what was that all about? I was in the bathroom and I heard *something*."

Ironically, that display of cowardice promptly resolved the issue.

COURAGE SEEN AS FOOLISHNESS

While filling a temporary sergeant slot on the swing shift, I responded to an incident. I was backing up the shift sergeant along with several others rather then directing the staff, so I had an opportunity to fully witness the incident rather then focus solely on the offender.

A tall, lean, muscular inmate with ham-sized fists was agitated. He had the kind of natural, tough build that indicated he could do incredible damage. His punch could crack a skull, break an arm, or dislocate a jaw. He wasn't a kid who was totally irrational or would easily back down, nor was he one of the weight pilers (serious weightlifters) who didn't know what to do with his strength. This guy moved like a fighter.

An officer who knew the inmate quickly filled me in. This was a tough con who knew the ropes and normally didn't get into trouble. For him to go off, something must have enraged him beyond what normally happened to inmates. He moved around the unit, threatening, defining his own perimeter by moving toward officers.

When dealing with an inmate who is going off like this, we don't force a physical confrontation more than necessary. We back off, but in the pack model, like wolves encircling a stag. He was feinting and moving forward, but we closed behind him as we moved up, his space getting smaller and smaller.

The shift sergeant continued his de-escalation techniques long past the point where I ignorantly assumed talking was over, but he had the advantage of having established a rapport with the con in the past. We maintained our perimeter and waited for the signal to take the guy down. In this case, the sergeant used good judgment. With a fighter like this inmate and with so many staff "up and ready," a scuffle would produce some injuries, with us hurting us more than us hurting him or him hurting us.

Suddenly, the inmate broke toward the door and went outside, stating that he'd walk on his own to the hole. I'd seen this before on graveyard shift; the inmate was simply walked down to segregation without cuffs and taken down in an area between two sets of sliders. It was all done out of the sight of other inmates so he didn't gain status by fighting us in front of others. I assumed we'd be doing that here.

An officer stood in his way. He held up his hand and blocked the con's progress.

"Get out of my way, old man," the inmate challenged, stopping.

"I can't let you go down the boulevard," the officer stated plainly, no hint of hesitation in his voice and no uncertainty on his face. He was ready to get into it.

"You better move. I'm going to walk to seg."

"No, you're going to listen to the sergeant," the officer continued.

The inmate flexed and slightly raised his balled fists. I figured the obstructing officer would take one good shot before we could stop the assault.

The exchange went back and forth, with the sergeant continually speaking to the offender. He eventually calmed down and didn't resist being cuffed, and the incident was resolved without anyone being hurt.

The other officers began calling the officer who stopped the inmate "Speed Bump" because they felt that he'd only slow down the inmate a second if he really wished to continue. But I had to follow up on what I saw. I didn't understand why the inmate wasn't simply allowed to continue to segregation.

I learned that the dynamics on swing shift were very different from those on graveyard in that too many inmates were awake and watching what took place. "Speed Bump" understood that if an inmate was permitted to set his own guidelines for going to the hole with so many others watching, we'd lose a tremendous amount of control. The officer so fully grasped the importance of maintaining what control we had that he was willing to absorb a serious punch to do so if necessary.

It took guts, but his only rewards were a cynical nickname from his peers—and my respect.

IGNORANCE SEEN AS COURAGE

I get to be a convenient example in my own book in the chapter on courage, but it's about perception equaling reality more then willful action on my part. On two occasions, acts based solely on my ignorance of situations benefited me.

I was still relatively new when an event that I didn't know was an event took place. After promising my then wife that I'd take one of the children to the doctor, I was "mandatoried," meaning I had to involuntarily work an eight-hour overtime commencing at the end of my shift because someone on the next shift wasn't there. It didn't matter what promises were made at home; the department had little sympathy for our private lives. Besides, I knew that if I didn't do it, someone else would have to, and the individuals next on the seniority list were my friends.

Two officers were assigned to the unit to which I was sent for my overtime shift, but both were already gone and my partner for that day hadn't arrived yet. I was alone in the unit with 100+ inmates until the shift sergeant and lieutenants unscrewed their rosters.

As I walked into the unit, I was surprised to find the televisions on since they weren't supposed to be that early in the morning. I was also surprised to find so many offenders in the dayroom at that time. The TVs, affixed high up on a support pillar in the center of the large room, were turned up too loud, and the inmates were competing with the volume.

I handled it as I had in the past. I grabbed the remote and shut down the televisions. I waited until every inmate in the room was looking at me, then got on the equivalent of a PA called a Stentophone.

"Alright, listen up. This unit is going to stay at a reasonable volume. If you try to compete with the TVs, I'm going to shut them down. If you try to compete with each other when talking, I'm going to clear the dayroom." I watched them glare at me, but they turned and began talking to each other quietly. The noise vanished, so I turned the televisions back on.

A large, muscular, black inmate, a tough guy known to many officers, approached me.

"I don't know how you feel about this, but I want to shake hands with the man with the biggest balls on the Island," he declared.

I shook his hand, figuring he was trying to play me and wondering what he was up to. Oddly, his tone was genuine, and he definitely didn't have a reputation as a leg rider.

"After yesterday, we were wondering how you all would react," he added, drifting back to his chair.

I shrugged it off as a weak manipulation attempt, and soon the shift sergeant arrived with my partner for the day.

"How's it going?" he asked.

"Not bad," I responded.

He turned to look at the inmates. "They acting any differently?"

I shrugged. "Inmates are inmates."

"That's good. Yesterday a bunch of them got out of hand and backed the officers in here up against the wall because one of them shut down the TVs. It could have gotten real ugly. I came up here to tell you to be careful; we dumped some of them, but we didn't get the ringleaders."

"Thanks," I said, restraining myself from adding, *"for telling me now!"*

In yet another irony of prison life, my ignorance was seen as courage by several inmates. I later learned that for a year, the same large con would walk up to other black inmates and warn them after they got into exchanges with me.

"You don't want to mess with that muthafucka [referring to me]. He's crazy and he don't give a shit. So he ain't impressed by how you're acting."

I didn't have many problems with black inmates that year.

A second example of ignorance perceived as courage also involved me. On this occasion, my partner grew restless just as I sensed something was going on in the unit. He told me that he was going to take batteries downstairs for the other officers' radios. I warned him that something was about to go down, but he left anyway.

A minute or so after he left, a tall, young inmate burst out of his room and sat at a table in the middle of the dayroom. His cellie, an older guy from Rykers Island across the country, came out and stood by the door, shouting at him.

"Come on back! You want to mess with an old man now, boy?"

"I ain't having none of that," the younger inmate responded.

I wondered what had happened. The younger guy appeared to be a scrapper who didn't seem like the type to back down. He was furious, but he didn't go after the much smaller, much older con.

"Come on *punk*, let's go!" shouted the old guy.

I moved up quickly, straight toward the agitator. The phone bank—a metal panel which held phones—was between us.

I addressed the younger inmate first. "You! Keep quiet. I'll handle this." He nodded in agreement and turned way. I turned to the older guy.

"Lock up!" I ordered.

"You gonna tell me to lock up when this is happening?"

"Lock up!" I repeated.

"You telling me to lock up with this all going down?"

"Lock up," I drawled so it would be very clear.

"What you gonna do with all this going down?"

"I'm going to lock you up," I said again, now getting irritated with the repetition.

He stared at me in disbelief, cursed at the younger inmate again, said something about everyone present having illicit arrangements with their mothers, and walked back to his room. I instructed the other inmate to stand by the sergeant's office, putting the whole dayroom between them, and called for the sergeant. Because it had only been a verbal exchange, I didn't bother clearing the other inmates from the dayroom.

After everything calmed down, one of my porters sauntered up.

"Man, I ain't seen nothing like that," he said.

"Yeah, old guy got mad; kid didn't want a part of it."

"Not that. *You went up against a man with a shank with nothing but a radio,*" he explained. "Come on. What you got on you? What you packing?"

If he was thinking I had pepper spray or an ASP baton hidden away, he was wrong. All I had was a Motorola and a cheap pen.

Shank! I never saw the weapon in the inmate's hand during the entire exchange.

I played it off.

"That's my job," I said.

I moved toward the room and looked in the window just in time to see the old con put something slim and shiny down a vent. He turned and grinned at me and dropped a toothbrush handle. I opened the door as back-up arrived, told him to move to the far end of the cell, and picked up the still warm handle. The smell of melted plastic filled the room.

"You ain't got shit on me," he stated.

Unfortunately, he was right. There was no way to retrieve the razor blade that comprised the business end of his now disassembled improvised knife. Higher-ups didn't see a shank as a shank when all they had as evidence was blunt, melted plastic. The inmate was dumped, but not for having a weapon or threatening anyone with one.

At least no one got hurt.

SMOKE, WATER, CHAOS

We moved about in the dark, dodging the piercing beams of expensive flashlights, screaming and rattling the chain-link placed to prevent inmates from being pitched over the railing. We responded to the lights by throwing water and debris and listened with uncontained rushes of adrenaline as large black forms moved up the metal steps, the fall of their heavy boots ringing in the darkness.

On that night, amid the screams of challenge and defiance from our raw lungs, in the smoke and dripping water, I was a rioting inmate.

I felt an odd mixture of heat and cold as I hid behind the jungle of cords, mattresses, and suspended bags and blankets on the third tier, standing beside the others, too excited and bellicose to care that we could only buy minutes against the inevitable. Our bravado couldn't last against the discipline, organization, and equipment being marshaled against us.

We heard them below and shouted mockingly as they slowly cleared the almost empty tier, with just one or two role players taking them all on and giving them a hell of a time. Then they were here—lights and shapes at the end of the narrow walkway, a threat bubbling up from the end of a long shaft. Reflections off face visors and shields marked their location. The long, narrow sheen off intimidating batons—36 inches of high-impact plastic designed specifically for inflicting pain—presented the real threat.

We rushed, then fell back. They swung at us and continued forward slowly, with organization, with a plan, while we merely reacted. I moved carefully at times, recklessly at others, kicking shields, throwing debris, watching the officers' defensive tactics, noting weaknesses. Finally, I rushed in and, with a young lieutenant temporarily demoted to rioting inmate, turned a man's shield as he broke ranks and made a grab for us. I literally climbed up between him and his shield and he went down. Then we introduced him to terror—and his peers to desperation—as we dragged him down the tier, over debris and damp mattresses, into darkness. A huge fellow "inmate" covered our withdrawal. Shouts of triumph alternated with coarse gasping and muttered curses.

We stripped the officer of his equipment, pummeling his armor and tearing the seat of his BDU trousers to give him a scare. He was stunned for a few seconds, then tried to fight back. But it was two on one, and his equipment now hampered him as we pinned him to the trash-strewn tier. We took his baton and helmet and raised them like trophies, shouting, challenging the others to break their ranks and come forward. We spent several more seconds standing before them holding up the helmet like a severed head, but we ran like mad when a shotgun was pointed at us, the message clear: they could have taken us down if they wanted to.

I volunteered to act as a rioting inmate as an experience, and I sure got one. I learned that my department had realistic training at levels I'd not seen in the army and only infrequently in the Marines. The realism really hit home when I was finally taken down and found a knee on the side of my head and, unfortunately, a sharp hunk of metal between my cheek and the concrete that left me with a jaunty cut. But no one was seriously hurt, and we all learned an incredible amount that no amount of classroom instruction could provide.

On the way out, I caught a ride with a bunch of officers who'd gone through the training on the other side, including one who complained that the seat of his pants had been ripped out by two guys who dragged him down the tier. I thought to myself that I was very, very glad to be backed up by these professionals. I could count on these people when I got into trouble.

SECTION 2

THE INMATES

5

The Hierarchy of Inmates

ust as there isn't any such critter as a typical Corrections officer, a typical inmate doesn't exist either. Despite this, officers categorize offenders all the time. We do it even at the risk of relying on base generalizations and making dangerous assumptions because it is a useful tool to convey essential information quickly and efficiently.

The population of a correctional facility *is* divided into strata and categories that both the staff and inmates recognize. Understanding the terms used to describe the various types of inmates is as important a piece of information as anything we are taught during training, yet many staff members don't use the terms properly because they don't know the distinctions.

An inmate refers to any offender, and inmates refers to the whole population, but specific terms refer to roles specific inmates fill. It's inappropriate to label an inmate incorrectly because it can lead to problems. For example, all cons are inmates, but in no way are all inmates cons. Hopefully the punks are all inmates, but in no way is every inmate a punk. Certain inmates are happier when simply referred to as inmate; others are outraged. An inmate will fight other criminals over being called a punk and will file a grievance if an officer calls him one. Certain things just aren't right, and calling an inmate a punk who isn't is a bad practice.

The following information refers mostly to male offenders. Specific divisions for female offenders are provided in Chapter 8. Interestingly, there aren't any female cons.

CONS

Cons are a distinct subgroup of inmates, and experienced staff members can recognize them. The term denotes a form of prison maturity and is almost respectful for those who understand the prison hierarchy.

While every offender might technically be an inmate, not all inmates are cons. Cons make up a distinct group with disproportionate power and influence within the system. They are older guys, at least in their thirties, and they have many years in the system. But time in doesn't indicate this status—most offenders today never get to the point where they are considered to be cons.

A con is an individual who knows how to do his own time, and he knows how to work the system. He is slick enough that we seldom catch him doing what he does best, which is conduct his illicit business in a low-key fashion. A con doesn't normally have to be corrected by a staff member if he is caught doing something. For example, offenders aren't supposed to sit on tables. If a con is sitting on a table, he'll get off before you see him, or he'll nod, smile slightly, and get off without your having to say anything. An inmate would need to be told to get off the table; a stupid inmate would argue with you. A con wouldn't be sitting on the table in the first place, or he wouldn't get caught for such a minor violation.

An example of a con I know is inmate Stable. I've known him for years, and he was already a con when I first entered Corrections. We seldom caught him doing anything, but one time during a random search we nailed him with a massive quantity of food stolen from the kitchen. I was surprised to catch him and I wondered how he'd take it. He chuckled, shrugged, and accepted responsibility without complaint. An inmate would have tried to lie, accuse others, and weasel his way out.

Cons can rival staff members in control of a facility. A unit with some cons in it is easier to run than a unit with only a few. A unit with many cons is dangerous because when enough of them are together, they get very, very organized and exert enough control to manipulate the whole group. Oddly, salty officers and, more frequently, sergeants and lieutenants sometimes work with cons to control a unit.

If a prisoner tells you, "I'm not an inmate, I'm a con," he generally is just an inmate. A con doesn't need to tell you who or what he is; you just know it. They obviously can be very dangerous individuals if they choose to be.

INMATES

The term "inmate" has two meanings. Primarily, it covers every offender in a facility. Technically, even cons are inmates. But it might also be used to label the vast majority of offenders who don't fall into any other general grouping in the hierarchy, which might not be such a place to be when you consider some of the other categories! As a group, it can include everything from killers to check kiters.

An inmate is someone who doesn't know how to do his time well and gets into trouble because of it. He lacks the guile and savvy of a con, so he makes mistakes and gets caught by staff and inmates. He hasn't matured in the system or established a reputation, nor does he have the respect of staff members or other offenders. In the modern era, the vast majority of prisoners are inmates.

STUPID INMATES

Some inmates are so unintelligent that there's no hope for them. They don't fall into any category of regular offenders, and it's arguable that they aren't exactly a minority among the population. Stupid inmates provide as much of a security threat as they do amusement, and I'm glad they lock them up.

The best way to describe these offenders is to tell you about some of them. One of the most interesting ones I met had gone from doing a few weeks on a trash detail for a county jail to being a long-term incarcerated prison inmate. The original beef stemmed from providing alcohol to underage drinkers, resulting in this rocket scientist being put out on the road with an orange vest, a pair of gloves, and a trash bag. He only had a few days to go when he received word that he'd miss a major kegger if he didn't get out that day. Not only did he decide to escape, but his strategy involved assaulting a staff member in the process. He was picked up at the party, charged, convicted, and put away, and continues to spend his time in prison. He's now in his late twenties. That can't-miss keg party cost him more than eleven years of his life.

I overheard a female offender boasting about her boyfriend to anyone who would listen. She was proud of him. He'd been offered a chance to trade several years for several months by going through a mild version of boot camp rehabilitation. Only one requirement: he had to have his hair cut. He said no. His hair was his *freedom*, and he wasn't going to give that up! He wound up with an additional three years of "freedom" in prison.

One day one of my more normal inmates, a college basketball player who got caught in a big scandal involving drugs and weapons, came out of his room. His state-issue pants were cut to just below his knee. It seemed his cellie had decided he didn't want to turn his trousers in to be hemmed in the sew shop, so he borrowed the scissors from the officer's station and started cutting. The only problem was, he and his cellie had the same waist size. Because the cellie didn't know which pants belonged to him, he cut them all because he wanted to make sure he got all of his.

The same scissors-happy inmate once boasted that he was actually a juvenile and that he'd outsmarted the system by being convicted under false ID. He figured that if he got caught again for a violent offense, he'd simply go under his real name and be a first-time offender. I reminded him that he'd be fingerprinted, and he couldn't reconcile that with a fake ID. He gulped. Then I thanked him and told him I'd be sending a memo to his counselor and that some other folks might want to talk to him.

Other bright boys aren't so amusing.

One guy killed an individual for one of those expensive leather jackets that were popular in the late 1980s and early '90s. Apparently he wanted one of the overpriced, multicolored pieces of crap but couldn't bring himself to work for one. How did they catch this criminal mastermind? There was blood on the jacket and a bullet hole through it, which he liked to show off to people.

Another kid was kind of pathetic. Seems that as a young teen he got another young teen pregnant. His reasoning skills were very limited and went something like this: "I got to work to get money. If I don't have money, the baby is hungry and cries. Tina gets mad when the baby cries."

Well, this guy has a problem with his car. He couldn't get the part he needed and he got into a confrontation with an employee in a shop. In his head, it became, "I got to work to get money. If I don't have money the baby is hungry and cries. Tina gets mad when the baby cries. If this guy hurts me, I can't work. I have to hurt him first."

Someone that dim might not belong in prison, but does he belong in public?

FIXATED INMATES

I have coined this term to describe those inmates who become wound up over something trivial until it becomes their world. Usually of average intelligence or above, these inmates do their time focusing on a very narrow aspect of the world, and nothing else matters. This becomes their freedom.

The object of their fixation is usually something harmless, such as cleaning tables. A fixated inmate will walk around ensuring they are clean. Then he will carefully position them, then clean them again. If you talk to him, he'll tell you precisely how many tables there are in the dayroom, and he can give you a history of repairs and the condition of each of them. He'll tell you what chemical is the best for cleaning, all the while staring at the tables with a spray bottle and a cleaning rag twitching in his hands.

Unfortunately, in Corrections there are individuals who can't stand to see anyone else happy. They play a dangerous game of trying to deny an inmate with a harmless fixation from fulfilling his need. I don't understand or appreciate this behavior—I consider the practice dirty, and the sly smirk of the type of officer who watches a frustrated fixated inmate is evil.

SCRAPS

A less common term used by a minority of inmates and damn few staff, a "scrap" describes a lowly type of inmate who everyone knows but who doesn't have a commonly accepted title. A scrap is a guy with no pride who begs from other inmates. Many were street people on the outside. They will do things like pull cigarette butts from butt cans, scrape out the filthy residue tobacco onto a "borrowed" piece of Zigzag rolling paper, and smoke it with a borrowed match. A typical scrap will have a shoe box holding such junk as a pencil, an empty cassette box, and two crumpled property receipts for a pencil and an empty cassette box.

For some reason, a scrap is not taken for a punk, and almost no one wants to harm him. Other inmates might have an odd affection for a scrap, giving him cigarettes, remnants of cans of soda, and other store items. Some inmates, of course, don't like them and call them names, but because others don't pick it up or respond well to it (unless the verbally assaulting inmate has some charisma), it's generally dropped.

Staff members with a nasty streak are much more likely to jokingly give a scrap a bad time in front of inmates, then give them something small like a stubby pencil or a book of matches. Once this occurs, the inmates take it as a sign that they, too, can mess with these unfortunates, and they turn the scrap into a pet by making him do tricks such as sing a song or do a dance for minor objects.

Scraps don't snitch, nor do they cause problems other than disturbing staff who can't stand the sight of a person rooting through trash. Their crimes vary widely, but none I've ever seen were violent offenders.

DINGS

Despite the tragedy of mental illness, the less-then-kind prison term for mentally ill inmates, "dings," somehow fits. The official term is "mentally ill offender," or MIO, but that term is used only in classes, on paper, or by those who specialize in this field (who think the term ding trivializes what they do, which isn't much if results are all that matters). Experienced staff and older cons use the term more frequently, but its use is fading as the blight of oversensitivity encompasses the field.

I once asked a con what his definition of a ding was after he used the term. He responded, "A ding is an inmate with mental problems so bad that if you had a six pack of them, you could walk 'em around and sell tickets to the freak show. That shit would be funny!"

The con's definition, while callous, clearly shows that dings are inmates with problems so pronounced that they are visibly noticeable. Mentally ill offenders might move awkwardly, wear clothing improperly, have problems with hygiene, or have slackened expressions. Some emanate a foul chemical stench, a result of the medications they take. Very noticeable is the "thyroxin shuffle," which is a slow gait caused by the effects of medication.

Sympathy toward mentally ill offenders often develops among the staff,

---

A Briefing on Mental Illness
"The use by a staff member of the term 'dings' to refer to the mentally ill members of our facility's population displays ignorance and insensitivity and is indicative of a callous attitude toward the less fortunate. The appropriate term is 'mentally ill offender' or, as written, 'MIO.'"
After a few seconds of guilty silence among the attendees, the smug instructor continued. "Now that that is clear, how do we identify these dings?"

as might be expected when dealing with anyone less fortunate, until you remember what they did to their victims. Bogus claims of mental illness made by defense attorneys also erodes the reception and treatment of the truly mentally ill by both staff and inmates.

The mental health staff at a correctional facility often has credibility problems in the eyes of the custody staff. We'd wonder how individuals, who made twice what we made and with all those years of education and practice, could make certain decisions about an inmate's status. I admit that we had an unsophisticated, pragmatic view. When I spoke with most of the shrinks, they proved to be intelligent people who were hampered by their own policies and procedures and faced pressures we didn't understand. What we also didn't understand was how much more unmanageable these inmates would be without the efforts of the mental health professionals.

Admittedly, dealing with the mentally ill offender was sometimes fascinating and frequently funny. This may sound harsh, but considering the alternating tedium and tension of a correctional environment, both staff and inmates keep an eye out for humorous things. An irrational inmate focused on an odd minor aspect of prison life has de-escalated more then one tense situation in prison.

Some behaviors are harmless, like the inmate who danced to the news, or the guy who kept smuggling in aluminum foil and wrapping it around his head to protect himself from alien or government beams that make the rest of us compliant. (Who knows? He might be right.) More than one had a cleaning fixation, and it was a blast to tell them that they missed a spot.

Because they require special handling, dings are labor intensive for the custody staff. A single MIO can cause more problems than any ten inmates. When a ding is wound up and about to go off (called "pinging"), he requires tremendous resources disproportionate to the population of offenders as a whole. Mr. Disco was a good example.

Mr. Disco believed we were still living in the 1970s. If he turned on the radio, he heard songs from the '70's (all disco) no matter what station it was on, and he'd talk about the new muscle cars. Around one in the afternoon, he'd get quiet and confused, and his living in the '70s abruptly ceased. I heard that he'd been hit in the head with weights or something in the big yard in the mid-1970s, and he simply replayed that day up to the point he got beaned by a bar. The inmates said, "He's the ding who got dinged!"

Mr. Disco would have a morning seizure and wind up on the floor twitching, but it was unique in that he could still talk to you. When this occurred, I'd calmly walk over, clear the area of other inmates and furniture, then grab a seat and talk to him, reassuring him that response was on the way. This kept him calm, and he seemed to do better if he could focus on someone's face and realize he was being taken care of. In short order, a sergeant, nurse, and several officers would arrive, per procedure.

Once we tried to estimate the cost of this inmate per year in manpower, as between response time and documentation it involved anywhere from 20 to 40 minutes per person from the sergeant, nurse, and three or four officers. When it got into the thousands, I dropped the calculation because I got the picture.

SNITCHES

Especially hated are the snitches, the inmates who feed information to staff on other inmate activities. The inmates despise them, although more than half will themselves snitch at some time. The staff despises them too, even though they can help us do our jobs more effectively and even save our lives. Many of the snitches despise themselves. But they are essential to the dynamics of a prison population.

In movies, a snitch is often depicted as a sneaky, socially awkward geek pushing a broom and looking about with shifty eyes as he passes information to an officer, who gives him a cigarette and sends him on his way. Sometimes he is portrayed as a likable, frail old guy who doesn't want something bad to happen, or maybe a weak, needy, fat guy with a squeaky voice. Normally the snitch is shanked or hung by other prisoners before the end of the flick.

As with most things in cinema, these stereotypes are partially accurate and enormously inaccurate. One common but little-known fact of prison life is that even tough, experienced offenders snitch. No matter who they are, once identified as a snitch (frequently incorrectly), the inmate will usually come forward and request protective custody. He will then be removed from the population and isolated from the other inmates in a small cell.

The most common snitch is a guy who considers himself clever and

---

The Peace Keeper and the Shank

A metallic clang sounded as a hairy hand pressed down on my desk near my arm. Astonished, I stared for a few seconds at eight and a half inches of tapered and sharpened steel, with a speckling of rust along the edge. This was a very impressive shank. An old con, looking damn serious, met my eyes with his burning visible through his stringy brown hair. In a low tone he said, "Mop closet upstairs. We don't need none of this shit in here. A man can't even clean his cell without having something like that fall out on him." He paused. "Give me at least five minutes to get away from here, and com'on, be low key."

I nodded. I was glad my partner was a mature, sharp guy who'd figure out the way we'd play this one. The shank was slid in the drawer as I talked to my partner. I waited a while, then sauntered over to the unoccupied sergeant's office with some files, one containing the improvised knife, where I made a call to the shift lieutenant.

We did a full-on search later during the shift, and I made a show of walking out of the area where the inmate reported he found the knife holding a paper sack. Only then did I bring the weapon to the shift office.

We later learned that a group of inmates, all dirtbag youngsters, had decided to make their bones by attacking an inmate they suspected of being a sex offender. Although the attack still occurred, it was with a much less lethal weapon, and no one was seriously injured. Serious injury or death was prevented by a snitch, not by officers.

An Odd Reassurance

As the prison population changes from inmates who mostly abide by the Convict Code to a collection of immature inmates with behavioral problems, a benefit toward staff safety has emerged: The vast majority of inmates will now snitch without much pressure. Many even volunteer information.

One day, a surly inmate was popping off and attempting to intimidate me after failing to get the response he wanted from making a direct threat. Although he was unwilling to go one on one, he continued his rant by reminding me that riots happen, and guys like me will "get yours."

I grinned at him and gestured to the many rooms around us.

"You'd have hundreds of eyes on you, all anxious, all taking in everything, and most of them belonging to snitches. You going to be able to shut up all the snitches? Would you go down for something another inmate did?"

He looked around, then sat down and became very quiet as he waited for the Quick Response Team to come pick him up.

---

believes there is power in feeding information both ways. I call them weasels, and I hold the actual smelly, skulking rodent in higher regard. The weasel will secure a job where he can gain access to staff members, such as a porter (janitor) or clerical position, so he can be seen talking to officers without arousing suspicion. From this position, he feeds info on staff members to the cons as frequently as he gives information on inmates to us. He revels in the role, not realizing the potential danger he is in, believing he is too useful to both the officers and the cons.

Because we know what they are and where their loyalties lie (with themselves), weasels are tolerated because they give us a better idea what is going on, and they provide an informal means to feed bullshit information to offenders who constitute more serious security concerns. Their information on fellow inmates is usually accurate, but it often covers minor things of limited value or is too vague or too late to be acted upon. They also run distraction or interference for the cons when something is going down. This is when they discover their true status with staff as we brush past them with impatience and contempt on our way to stop whatever it is they are trying to cover for.

One of the weasels in my unit was a porter who provided information of limited value. Inmate Sleazy let me know that over the weekend, someone got punked in the bathroom, but he didn't know who or by whom, or that the guy who'd just been released kept a shank in his sock. He never provided anything of value until we caught him on a major infraction and pressured him to give up good information on who was smoking marijuana. Three inmates were caught in subsequent urinalysis (pee tests for illicit substance consumption).

The peace keeper snitch is much more valuable. This guy doesn't usually make it his job to be a snitch, but he'll give precisely accurate information on the illicit activities of other inmates when decisive action is essential. He simply wants to do his time without problems in his unit or area, and he doesn't want his own illegal activities interfered with. Some of these guys touch base with officers periodically in casual, acceptable conversations so that when they do snitch, nothing unusual is suspected. A peace keeper once gave up a female staff member who'd gotten too close to an inmate. She was white, the inmate black; too many of the inmates were pissed at the situation, the snitch explained, and trouble was brewing.

One of my best peace keepers was a convicted murderer with more years in the system then some staff members had on Earth. A personable guy, he wanted to do his time in quiet, conducting his own nefarious business discreetly. He disliked the gangbangers and the peckerwoods who stirred things up in the unit.

Over the years he provided great information, especially on staff misconduct that might have caused serious problems. He told me very important information, almost all of which involved potential violence, which I passed on up my chain and to my peers.

Did I ever trust him? No. Did he ever get a break from me because he was a good snitch? He thought he did.

A common form of snitching that's not considered snitching is "dry snitching," which has two definitions. The first is when the staff is given incorrect information just to manipulate them. The other form is when accurate information is passed by inmates who are "overheard" by the staff. They talk a little bit louder than they should or use a tone that attracts attention as they discuss other inmates. Dry-snitched information can be exceptionally useful or totally valueless, but generally, based on the situation we know which it is in minutes.

Some individuals who aren't true criminals (in that they didn't pursue a life of crime but in a moment of weakness or stupidity committed a felony) frequently snitch when they see something wrong, such as a punk being turned out or strong-arming taking place. These guys are exceptionally valuable because they put the information down on paper. Unfortunately for them, because they don't know the Convict Code, they do it in front of other inmates. We generally protected these guys, but they were one-shot deals because their astonishment at the reaction of the other inmates taught them not to do it in the future.

Interestingly, cons do a great amount of snitching but are never suspected or questioned by the population except in extreme situations, as they are established and often too dangerous to slap a snitch jacket on.

SEX OFFENDERS

Sex offenders are held in low regard by all the other inmates. When an inmate suspects another of being a sex offender, the common challenge is,

The Sisterhood

In the movie *The Shawshank Redemption*, "the Sisters" referred to a group of predatory, homosexual rapists. Twisting it a little, I found it to be the perfect description for a group of inmates I dealt with during a tense period in my unit. I called them "the Sisterhood."

In the movie—which, by the way, contains some of Hollywood's worst depictions of correctional staff (though possibly accurate for the period)—there is a horrifying series of scenes showing a group of vicious homosexual rapists who prey upon the protagonist until he learns how to work the system and get a payback. While not as common in modern facilities due to heavier staff involvement, better security coverage, and the willingness of inmates to snitch, packs of predatory homosexual rapists do exist.

The Sisterhood in my facility was composed of three lean, muscular inmates with uniquely hard looks for young men. As an example of their behavior, I once observed them prowling around an incoming chain. They quickly focused on a rather young man with flowing blonde hair. What was unsettling was the manner in which they displayed their intent. They openly moved in on this oblivious fellow, despite the fact he wasn't small or weak, with the staff right there observing them. While one engaged the target in conversation and offered him a cigarette, the others stood behind him, checking him out as openly as Marines check out bar girls in Tijuana.

While the Sisterhood was in the unit, I prayed we wouldn't have a riot! They seldom sat together but instead took positions around a room, communicating with glances and signals. Eventually we were able to break them up.

"Let me see your papers," referring to his legal paperwork, which may include his charge sheet. To many inmates, this is seen as an accusation that they are child molesters, and I've had to break up heated exchanges over this issue.

Contrary to popular belief, sex offenders don't face the fate depicted in the movies and on television. Rather than being the recipient of nightly beatings and worse, the reality is that they are protected. As correctional officers, it was our responsibility to look after their safety, repugnant as it seems. We had to remind ourselves that we were not there to punish anyone.

I originally figured sex offenders would be low-key and easy to deal with because they were supposedly so threatened, but I found the opposite to be true. Among male offenders, there is no bigger group of whiners. Every minor medical problem is a crisis in their eyes, and their-self-obsessed personalities and constant petty complaints are almost catered to, if not always acted upon.

Think about it. Anyone who would hurt a woman or child is so self-involved that they believe the whole world revolves around them. I base this opinion not on an emotional response to their crimes but instead on years of watching them and listening to their complaints. They ask for favors and other things with childish greed and directness. If they are entitled to something, they make sure they get it, even if they don't need it right then. They are pathetic human beings.

Although rapists and child molesters (including sexually motivated killers) are both categorized as sex offenders and share some traits, there are differences between the two.

Child Molesters

Also called "Chesters" (as in "Chester the Molester"), child molesters have a precarious position in a correctional facility. Druggies keep to themselves—they've been avoiding authority figures and other squares for years. Many violent offenders are independent and lone-wolf types, and other inmates have their subgroups and gangs for support. Exposed child molesters are often left on their own, and the only folks around who won't potentially attack them are the staff. Some have developed amazing levels of cultural assimilation to conceal their crimes, and when I was new I sometimes wondered why certain guys were in prison until I figured them out.

Although they are extremely self-involved like all sex offenders, Chesters on average make for surprisingly good, manageable inmates in the short term. They often prove to be hard workers as unit janitors because it provides them with a form of approval. Many are good snitches, and they can be easy to "work" from an officer or sergeant's point of view, but in the long term, they get irritating with their constant whining.

Rapists

Rapists are different from child molesters in several ways. They have a more predatory appearance even in a correctional facility, and they are more threatening to both male and female staff. They are much more willing to use violence than a cowardly child molester, who is more into deception and persuasion. More than one young inmate has assumed that a rapist was an easy target for assault because he was a sex offender. This is especially stupid when one considers that rapists often have spent time in hard-core prisons and faced shit that would have turned the wannabe tough guys into screaming punks.

The intellect and sociability of rapists ranges from brilliant to inbred cretins. In my experience, they can be more dangerous to staff members, male and female, than any other type of inmate (especially if they have mental problems) because when they get worked up, they want to enforce their will on others no matter what. If an inmate is both a sexual predator and severely mentally ill, he is an extremely dangerous individual with a high potential for violence.

PUNKS

Punks occupy the lowest strata of the inmate population. It is the first term to learn and the one that requires the most care when using in a prison. A punk, in the definitions of both staff members and inmates, means an inmate who is sexually used by other inmates. Whether this is a willingly accepted role or not is incidental—a punk is a punk.

When a fresh kid comes in as a "fish," or a new inmate, and is first used as a punk, or when he's set out as a punk by an older, stronger inmate (usually a con), it's called "turning out." Frequently, we attempted to prevent young, weak inmates from being turned out, making it known to the "cell daddy" that the activity wasn't tolerated.

Often, an inmate who was a full-out punk at a previous facility wanted to change how he did his time. Unfortunately for him, there are always enough felons around who would remember him as a punk, so word would get out and predators attracted. Some fall back into the role with little pressure; others resist even intense pressure. This leads to problems, because some predators won't take no for an answer. For many, the attitude is once a punk, always a punk. It's something they can't leave behind as long as they're in the system.

Although I learned to have contempt for punks and their weak personalities, as a correctional officer I had a responsibility to protect them. When we protected a punk, he sometimes wanted to become *our* punk, but not in the same way. He would do things such as give us information or do cleaning or other jobs around the unit. For the most part, we didn't want them around.

Race

elcome to a flash point in the field of Corrections. Even though it may be politically incorrect to say so, it is a fact that race is an important factor among the inmate population. Some staff members avoid the topic simply because to discuss it requires gross generalizations at some level, and that can be seen as incorrect or offensive. Perhaps others avoid the issue because it is very complex. Whatever the official case may be, race in prison simply cannot be ignored or denied.

Race is an immediate and obvious division that provides identity and a sense of security for some offenders. Furthermore, almost all inmates base many of their actions upon expectations of peers from their racial groups. Ignoring this fact of prison life is dangerous, because it prevents a necessary, fuller understanding of prison dynamics.

Beyond basic racial divisions, there exist rough subgroups within each group that can be used to define an offender more specifically and convey information that is in some ways useful for correctional officers and staff. It is controversial to label people in this manner, and some view it as dangerous and deceptive because there are continual exceptions, but a reality of Corrections is that such divisions and stereotyping is relied upon everyday by staff and inmates alike.

THE WHITES

The majority of the white offenders don't belong to the specific groups in this section, but after taking out the cons, snitches, punks, dings, druggies, and the categories that follow, there aren't that many of them left. Interestingly, among the prison population nationwide, Caucasians still form the largest single racial group behind bars.

Career Criminals

The old, regular career criminals—those involved in swindles, armed robberies, and the types of crime featured on the old "Dragnet" TV show—are becoming scarcer in prison, or perhaps it only appears that way as the numbers of other types swell. There are African-American career criminals in prison, but at one time it was the predominant type of white inmate.

Like cons, the career criminal is a diminishing breed, one which will always be there but as a smaller percentage of offenders. As the focus of law enforcement fell on more violent and sexually motivated criminals, and as the drug war continued to fill prisons with dealers and users, the number of career criminals was reduced in proportion and their time spent behind bars became shorter. They are more common in jails, where they serve a year or less for misdemeanors that were once considered felonies.

For correctional staff, career criminals are often easy to work with. One unit janitor I supervised was a career criminal who had served federal time for bank robbery. He was an incredibly hard worker and kept to himself. I asked him why he just didn't work as hard out on the streets. He grinned and said, "I do, but it's in cons, robbing, and stealing." We never caught him doing anything illicit. He just wanted to get back on the streets and go back into business.

Peckerwoods

Though often not from rural areas, peckerwoods are self-proclaimed "good ole boys." They are not frequently identified as a group, although the type of inmate is common. Taking great pride in being called peckerwoods or hicks, these individuals are generally seen wearing baseball caps over long or short hair and, if permitted, will opt for tank tops or roll their sleeves up higher than normal. They may even adopt twangs—exaggerated if they actually come from a region where a twang is common, faked if they're from areas where they aren't. They are on the fringe of the "white pride" group but aren't necessarily racists.

Skinheads

Skinheads constitute the lowest rung of the racist white inmates. Ranging from scrawny, pimply youngsters to psychotic tough guys, indications of abuse and neglect earlier in their lives are common among these very angry young men. Skinheads are usually violent, but they prey only on the very weak and generally on other whites, as any group of black inmates is more likely to be in better shape (most of these guys don't have the discipline to lift weights) and more able to scrap with them. Unfortunately, enough of them are big and tough enough that they can be dangerous. One of the rougher ones I dealt with attempted to organize a group in my unit. He'd been shipped out of another facility for participating in a real nasty incident, and he'd spent his time in the Intensive Management Unit. When he came out of the hole with a reputation and a following, he was heading toward becoming a problem.

With the guidance of a very experienced, older officer, now deceased, I was able to diminish the inmate's power play while serving as a temporary sergeant. The experienced officer, an African-American, said that it was essential that the staff show unity and told me that the racial mix of swing shift officers in the unit could be used to defeat the organization of the skinheads.

One of the actions I took was suggested by the old-timer after I had a confrontation with the skinhead. I'd given him an opportunity to take off the white shoelaces in his highly shined black boots in his room, but he came out and stared at me defiantly. We figured he had his chance, so I did it on front street—with back-up standing by out of sight, I made him cut them off in the dayroom. It had a tremendous effect on his status among the other offenders.

But the single most effective technique that finally beat the problem skinhead was a simple response to an insulting comment he made to the old-timer. Rather than becoming angry, the officer simply laughed and gave the inmate a friendly pat on the ass as he passed in front of the other offenders in the dayroom. Although I thought it was a mistake, the result was that the skinhead was completely discredited as the end-all of violent racism in the unit. Everyone from the hardened Aryan Brotherhood to the militant Muslims snickered at him. Only after I cleared the paperwork on that grievance did the old-timer wink, and then I understood—it wasn't an accident.

Aryan Brotherhood

The Aryan Brotherhood refers to members of the prison gang of that name or individuals affiliated with it on the outside. The Aryans generally have long hair, unkempt beards and mustaches, and tattoos of swastikas, skulls, and/or, cloverleafs. (The first time I saw one, I thought, 4H?) The AB is often allied with Native American inmates, especially nosebleed Indians (more on them later).

ABs might not necessarily conduct themselves as pure racists, as many of them joined the gang for mutual protection. Some don't hold racist views other than those directly relating to prison survival; others are worse than Nazis. Interestingly, some ABs feel a special repugnance for the upstart skinheads, who they view as punks and kids.

Neo-Nazis

In this category I'm not including skinheads who claim to be Nazis. I am talking about a much more narrow and sophisticated group. Constituting well-organized, trained, and committed racists, neo-Nazis are far fewer in number than Aryans or skinheads. These individuals have a neater appearance, and most held skilled jobs with decent pay on the outside.

I only saw one neo-Nazi in my time in Corrections. Self-disciplined, savvy, and very intelligent, his control and subtle means of exerting influence made him potentially more dangerous than the Aryans and definitely more so than the skinheads. He was driven and focused, and the only indication we had of his racist views came from his reading material, his veiled expressions, and an occasional restrained smirk. I was concerned he was going to manipulate the skinheads, but he dismissed them as punks. Fortunately, true neo-Nazis, as opposed to glorified skinheads, are rare.

Constitutionalists

Constitutionalists, such as the Freemen of Montana, are individuals who are steeped in their version of the U.S. Constitution. Mistaken for militia members, these folks are more into paperwork then weaponry.

Angry oratory best describes them, because given an opportunity they well spout off on how our rights have been taken, the evil of a gold fringe on the American flag, and a host of other things. They claim not to recognize the validity of the courts that convicted them or even of the current U.S. government. For some reason they definitely accept the validity of its currency, as most of them are in for defrauding the government or fellow citizens.

I confronted one of these yahoos once and had the tremendous satisfaction of dicing him to pieces in a debate on Constitutional rights and the Federalist Papers. I had just happened to have brushed up on my reading on those topics days earlier. It was a, uh, coincidence.

Eastern Blockheads

The number of inmates from the former Eastern Bloc nations (Russia, Poland, Bulgaria, etc.) grows as the population of immigrants increases and the organized crime from that region shifts to the United States. Though few in number, these inmates are growing as a group. Extremely bullheaded and aggressive, they are a significant problem in East Coast and Midwest facilities.

Eastern Blockheads are interesting in that they laugh at our form of corrections. Compared to where they'd been, incarceration in our worse prisons is easy time to them, so it isn't a deterrent to their criminal behavior. I remember ane inmate from one of the former Soviet Republics who told me that the food he ate in prison was better than any he ate at home, in or out of prison. He couldn't believe we heated the living units on mildly cold days, that the water was so clean, that he was issued new clothing, and that he could do so many things. In many ways, he was more free as a prisoner in the United States then he was as a citizen before the collapse of the Soviet Union. He was a very hardened and jaded individual for such a young man.

Biker Dudes

Burly, bearded, and dirty, these guys look like bikers so much that I envision them as wearing their colors even when they are in prison blues or khakis. They feel as if they have to display a picture of a Harley Davidson motorcycle in their cell, and they know that many officers are in to Harleys too. After checking into many of the biker dudes, I've learned something interesting: Many never really owned bikes. In fact, most weren't affiliated with biker gangs, and the second a real biker came into the unit, they put in a lot of cell time.

Wannabes

Wannabes are white inmates who act as if they are members of African-American culture. They are held in universal contempt by staff and inmates, both black and white. Because they are seen as weak and without self or ethnic pride, black inmates use them for everything. Some of these kids actually come from decent families, and they use the money their parents send them to keep gangbangers in candy bars, sodas, and smokes. Wannabes see this as acceptance.

THE BLACKS

Like their Caucasian counterparts, African-American inmates fall readily into more distinct groups, with numerous exceptions. This again is a form of stereotyping for convenience, but after removing the drug addicts, sex offenders, cons, punks, and dings, you're left with a sizable number of inmates who fit in the following categories.

Original Gangstas

Also called Original Gangsters and OGs, these are generally black offenders who come from places like the Compton and Watts areas of Los Angeles. OGs are experienced gang members who generally have "earned their bones" (i.e., they've killed or badly hurt someone) and have established themselves in their set.

Because they are established in the prison population, OGs have power and influence among other gang members. In a way, some OGs are like cons in that they will manipulate younger, stupider, and less mature offenders to get things done while they stay clear of obvious involvement. Their main concern is to get back on the street and back to dealing drugs, living what they see as the good life of chasing tail and driving fine cars for the short periods between stints in prison.

I once spoke with an OG about his view on prison when I was going through his property to check for contraband, and here's what he said: "I got pull [power] on the outside and on the inside. I got money and juice and I got my bitches on the outside and the inside. Ain't no difference being here or being free."

Gangbangers and Wannabes

Members of the infamous Bloods and Crips gangs might be of any race, but they are dominated by African-Americans. The Black Gangsta Disciples are definitely an African-American group.

Many young, inexperienced gang members are more eager to prove themselves and are much less mature and patient than OGs. They are dangerous in the streets and stupid-dangerous inside because they are so into the image of the thug life that they don't see the futility of their actions. They are more into banging than business. This is why so many young black men are tragically killing themselves.

Some inmates can be categorized as gang wannabes. They remain on the fringe of the gangsta life without real affiliation or commitment because they're either not wanted or they don't want to be jumped in (think very rough hazing). Although a trend in law enforcement is to not make distinctions between gang "associates" and the real deal, in their world there *is* a difference between someone who's in a set and someone who's a "weak assed punk muthafucka wannabe."

A perfect example of a wannabe was an African-American inmate named Cole. Cole caught my attention because he bore many gang-related traits. He spoke the street too keenly, knowing every term and salting his dialogue with them for emphasis. He wore the stocking cap pulled down and had the strut just right. He sagged his pants, held the right expression of irritated, mocking defiance, and tried to associate with the "right" offenders. But Cole had selected an appearance of the thug life but didn't actually want to live it. His most serious offense was defiantly popping off at officers who, unlike inmates, wouldn't pummel his scrawny face. While searching his property, I was surprised to find photos of his home and family. He came from a largely white family in an expensive neighborhood. He'd grown up with a boat and a new pick-up truck. He'd gone to private school and, judging from his paperwork, was articulate and very intelligent. Several inmates hated him because he didn't have "street authenticity." They were real gangbangers, and they introduced him to the thug life enough to damage some very expensive orthodontic work and put a scar under one eye.

Daddies

Not affiliated with gangbangers, daddies are older black males who think they are "playas." Some are pimps; some are wannabe pimps (or Mac Daddies). Generally they aren't any trouble for staff members, although some can be an annoyance or, at worst, stalker of female staff members.

Muslims

After taking a few years of Islamic cultural studies at the University of Washington and doing my own "know your enemy" research while serving in the Marines, I learned something quickly. The Nation of Islam—the black American Islamic group—practices a very, very different form of the religion than Arabic and Balkan Muslims. It's so different that a confused Muslim inmate from the Balkans once approached me after a Nation of Islam service and asked where the Islamic service was being held because he'd missed it.

Be that as it may, the Islamic inmates are generally better groomed than average and carry themselves with some dignity. They do not mind the fact that they appear scholarly, whereas others might consider them to be Uncle Toms for being bookish. They can be very well organized, and they hold court among themselves. I suspect that they might work with the Aryan Brotherhood to respectively police their own ranks, i.e., punish their own members who cause problems rather than allow AB on Muslim or Muslim on AB violence.

Deacons and Holy Rollers

Not to be confused with genuine Christian inmates, some inmates, race incidental, act as the proverbial Bible thumpers. The black ones are more noticeable to me because they usually get into bitter arguments with each other, whereas the white ones got along well enough or were solitary and individually stranger by comparison. These inmates attempt to use scripture and cite verses that even religious officers can't find in their Bibles. We figured if it's loud and profane, it's bogus; if it's quiet and profound, it's possible.

Scholars and Booker Ts

Every now and then we came across black offenders who approached time in prison in the manner most college students should approach their studies. They tried to learn everything. It's a tough fight for many, as some inmates, especially the gangbangers, give them a bad time and try to take them down. Unfortunately, some go off on a destructive, anti-white, anti-establishment slant, but others don't. They genuinely try to make something of themselves. They're known as scholars or "Booker Ts" after Booker T. Washington, an inspirational black educator and leader who founded the Tuskegee Institute in Alabama, advised American presidents, and still serves as a role model to some offenders.

Once I had a chilling experience when I was outside of an all-night convenience store. Someone called out behind me, "Officer Martin." Since most officers call me Martin, Marti, or Tom, it had to be an inmate. I turned and was relieved to see inmate Thomas standing near a car full of wholesome-looking kids.

"I wanted you to know, I'm doing as I said," he stated. "I have a job and I'm getting As at Pierce College. We're not all bad."

He's right. I remembered Thomas. He spent his spare time teaching other inmates how to read and get their GEDs. He was a natural leader, and I'd wondered what he was doing in prison because he didn't seem like a criminal.

Word is, he wasn't—except for lying in court. He took his brother's beef because he had a clean record and his brother would have gone down for a much longer time. Thomas stepped up and "confessed." His brother was on the verge of "straightening himself out," and Thomas wanted to give him enough time to do it even if it meant a sacrifice of years. My contact in the school district confirmed that everyone was shocked that this scholar-athlete confessed to a crime.

If this had been Hollywood, his brother would have used that chance to straighten his life out, and somehow Thomas would have gotten that university scholarship he probably sacrificed.

But this isn't a movie script. His brother went out and committed other crimes. When he was caught, they found him using his incarcerated brother's ID.

Inner City Intrigue

A conspiracy theory held by some black inmates (and many others) is fascinating and would be great plot material for a movie. The theory is that consortiums of businessmen and community leaders deliberately work to break down an inner city neighborhood in order to lower property values so they can buy real estate at bargain prices; then they ram an urban renewal plan through to jack up the prices and lure growth.

To accomplish this, "They" limit police coverage in an area, or ensure that response time is very slow. Because this mysterious, powerful group controls the media, crime in the neighborhood is always sensationalized and widely covered. Eventually, everyone outside of the afflicted region associates its name with high crime and tries to avoid it, with the exception of those seeking crack and weed.

Businesses in the area are shaped according to this nefarious plot: grocery stores are driven out while small mom-and-pop shops charging incredible prices are allowed to thrive. In this area of town, a 40-ounce bottle of Old English malt liquor costs very little, while a loaf of bread is much more expensive. Drugs are available inexpensively on the corners, and guns are plentiful and amazingly cheap. Community leaders who attempt to make changes are discredited; many become the victims of police sting operations.

After the property prices have dropped low enough and the consortium has purchased enough land, the swing of the pendulum begins to take place. News articles about the area abound about the "rejuvenation" of the city core. Reports of crime and violence diminish in the media, which is no surprise because police coverage increases dramatically. Politicians make promises that are actually kept, and big renewal projects are announced. Sometimes it's so blatant that ads inviting businesses into the area appear in the same newspaper issue that proclaims a dramatic revival of the formerly rundown region of the city.

Then another lower to middle income minority neighborhood in another city slowly begins to deteriorate . . . .

I really, really hope this is just an interesting but groundless conspiracy theory.

Race Riot

One day, while working in the kitchen on overtime, I walked out back where the inmates unloaded trucks and smoked or slacked off. From inside the building I looked out and saw several of them totally engrossed while staring at the sky, shouting encouragement such as, "Get that muddafucka!" and "Nail that bitch hard!"

Figuring there was a fight in progress on some roof or in some room visible through a window, I called out to the nearest officer, ran out the door, and found that the inmates were definitely watching a terrible fight—but they were cheering on seagulls and crows as they fought for turf in the sky above the Dumpster. I realized the black felons were rooting for the crows while the white offenders supported the seagulls, but it was being done in good humor.

After a while, the fighting broke off as several seagulls swept into the area and numbers won out. One of the guys turned toward me and said, "Sergeant, who do you back?"

The gathered inmates grew silent, waiting for my response.

"Cats," I quipped, going back inside.

THE HISPANICS

The label "Hispanic" is as deceptive as white or black, because it could lead to gross assumptions regarding these offenders. Hispanic inmates are a diverse group, with a lot of variety among what are commonly identified as Hispanic groups and individuals. Because being able to speak Spanish and having certain racial characteristics aren't requisites to being considered Hispanic, it can be a broader term than black or white. Individuals lumped in this category can include blacks, whites, and Indians as well as those of mixed Spanish and Indian heritage.

Mexicans

Not too long ago, the difference between Mexican inmates from Mexico and Mexican-American inmates was easy to see in how they kept their rooms. If it was a Spartan room with few personal goods, decorated with improvised craft items such as picture frames made with Mylar weaving, and had a picture of the Virgin Mary or Jesus on the bulletin board near a photo of a plain, brightly smiling woman and several children, you knew you had an illegal who came north to deal heroin.

For a while, most of the Mexican nationals we saw were family men who got caught moving drugs. These guys were hard-working porters who generally didn't treat staff members with disrespect. We had the impression that they had taken a calculated risk and lost and were willing to live with the consequences.

But those days have changed now that the drug trade has become more sophisticated. The number of Mexican inmates from rural areas who were hard workers before they drifted into dealing black tar and grass has decreased. They've been replaced with a harder group of Mexican offenders, more violent, more direct in attempts at manipulation, and with less patience. One offender told me that these "new guys" are more from border areas and urban centers who came up north specifically to commit crimes. I remember one inmate who was getting out. Unlike most of the other Mexicans in the unit, he was one of the new hardened criminals. Before he was handed over to the Immigration and Naturalization Service (INS) to be deported, he said to me, "You're next day off is Saturday. I'll be back up in Seattle before you will."

He was right, and Seattle was only about 40 miles away.

Mexican-Americans

Sophisticated and savvy or bullheaded and pugnacious, the Mexican-Americans who hadn't been anglicized were mostly gang members with histories of violence or simply Hispanic-Americans who were not too culturally different from the bulk of the population. What I found interesting was the fact that Mexican-Americans and Mexican nationals kept apart when there were enough to populate two separate groups. They appeared to have more scorn for each other then others did for either group.

It seemed the more savvy and acculturated the individual inmate, the quicker he was to claim he was being discriminated against because he was Hispanic. One claimed that the only reason he was being held accountable for his actions was because he was Hispanic. Ironically, the officer he was complaining to was a Mexican-American from California with a Hispanic name.

Cubanos

In 1980, President Jimmy Carter let Fidel Castro open up his prisons and psychiatric wards and dump vermin and sociopaths on this country. The remnants of the boatlift refugees still appear in prisons, and I had the experience of dealing with a few of these stubborn, difficult inmates. These guys were too angry to even smirk. Like the Eastern Blockheads, we couldn't do anything to them that they couldn't take. They saw us as relative amateurs in punitive actions.

Mainstreamers

Some Hispanic inmates, like many Hispanics in the population, are what is called "mainstreamed." They are more closely tied to standard American middle class values and lifestyles, or they identify with American culture as a whole more than any distinct Hispanic culture. They might be of Mexican, Cuban, or Puerto Rican descent. A derogatory term for mainstreamers is "Anglicized," as in they've become white.

THE ASIANS

Small in numbers, Asians are a mixed and not very unified group in prison. Whereas members of the previous racial groups often show some cohesion within prison, Asians are distinct in that many don't overemphasize their racial identity beyond specifics like their country of origin.

Innate to many Asian inmates, especially first- or second-generation Americans, is a sense of having failed if they've been incarcerated. It might seem ignorant or archaic to use a term like "loss of face," which doesn't exactly equate to "shame," but it can be applicable when dealing with some Asian offenders.

Southeast Asians

Most of the Vietnamese, Cambodians, and Laotians I encountered were in for violent offenses. They had little acculturation and a great amount of rage. Most were small sons of a bitches, especially compared to the blacks and whites, and they hung together closely for protection and because of their cultural distinctions. As a result, most weren't too much of a problem but the exceptions really stood out. Inmate Hao, for example, lunged through some bars and battered an offender twice his size and strength because of an insult to his sister. We'd been warned about another Southeast Asian offender who'd killed someone out on the streets for a perceived dismissive look. If he threatened you, he meant it and he would definitely act, which wasn't common among inmates.

Koreans and Japanese

Darn few Koreans and Japanese are in American prisons, except perhaps in Hawaii, where the latter forms a significant portion of the population. It's interesting to note that as powerful as the Korean mob is (run largely by former ROK soldiers), so few of them are imprisoned in the United States. Most of the Koreans I encountered were involved in graft; most of the Japanese-Americans were in for violent offenses or had stolen a tremendous amount of money.

For members of these two groups, being in prison is an incredible loss of face and a disgrace to their families. Many act as if they are humbled or disguise their background by blending in with the Native Americans.

Chinese

Chinese and Chinese-Americans are in prison for a wide range of criminal activity, from petty crimes to mass murder. They form a bit larger group than the Koreans and Japanese but are not a very big group as a whole. They have a long history in the American criminal justice system because they've been in this country for so long, with some of them winding up in prison almost immediately. While perusing reproductions of inmate records from the 1800s, Chinese faces and names appeared not so infrequently, whereas few other Asian groups were represented that far back.

NATIVE AMERICANS

I'd doubt a survey would be allowed, and it's considered offensive and politically incorrect to question someone's stated racial identity, but huge numbers of inmates who claim to be Native Americans simply are not. Many of these individuals are what others call "nosebleed" Indians, meaning that with one nosebleed, they'd be white. In fact, in some facilities, the majority of Native Americans are Caucasians—blond-haired, blue-eyed Indians—who either claim dubious links to Native American tribes or became interested in Native American religion while not portraying themselves as being anything other than that. The genuine Indians viewed the others with anything ranging from hostility and contempt to warmth and acceptance.

The center of Native American life in prison is the sweat lodge, a space that belongs to them and is generally left alone by non-Indians and staff members. Control of the sweat lodge, rituals, and sacred items is sometimes a source of conflict, most commonly between purists and those who seek to use these things for defeating security at the facility.

One of the best means I had to gain respect among the Native Americans was to show respect when dealing with their ceremonies and religious items.

Meet Some of the Boys

To give a more personal glimpse of the inmate population, here are the stories of several individuals I remember well who were all in my unit at roughly the same time. They include a drug dealer, a mentally ill offender, a remorseful murderer, and a crew of offenders who actually became a team. I remember them because they aptly illustrate what some offenders are like, what it's like to deal with them, and how interesting some of them are to observe.

MR. PRESCRIPTION

We had an inmate in my unit who one of the Response and Movement officers (R&Ms) called "Mr. Prescription" because he dealt drugs and could get anything the offenders needed. He was well known to the security staff as a dealer, but they never caught him. At best, they caught one of his mules who was holding for him but wouldn't admit it. If I used his real name, officers who knew him who are reading this book would say, "Oh, yeah, *that* son of a bitch."

This cocky inmate was a muscular black guy with a broad, gap-toothed grin and strong gang ties, although I don't think he was jumped in with the Crips. He liked being the focus of our attention. He'd strut around the unit with a do rag on his head, black and tied back, his khaki shirt and trousers always ironed even though we never lent him an iron. For the most part he avoided us and didn't do any dealings in the unit that we knew about, or so we thought. Swing shift searched his room as much as any other and found nothing. We pat searched him a bit more randomly than others and came up with negative results as well.

One day, we received a kite from an inmate that told us that the way to catch Mr. Prescription was to wait until he had a drug deal just about to happen, because in prison the risk was in getting caught carrying, not in the actual exchange. The inmate informed us that Mr. Prescription wouldn't have the contraband on him until just before delivery. Apparently, he liked to do the exchanges himself, because this way he knew he wouldn't get burned by one of his middlemen and could be certain the delivery was made. He also probably liked the feeling of power when he handed over what someone else needed so badly.

With this in mind, my partner of the month—a female officer who I really didn't like and who didn't like me, but we worked well as a team—dedicated a great amount of time trying to watch Mr. Prescription covertly. We didn't have any luck, until one day an inmate I'll call the Weasel attempted to interest me with what he'd heard the Mexicans were doing in the yard. I pretended to focus on him, knowing that he was running distraction for a reason.

We'd already caught on that something big was going down, because a group of white, predatory, homosexual rapists (the ones I called the "Sisterhood") and a few Aryan Brotherhood members were on one side of the dayroom (an unusual combination unless something big was in the offing), and the Crips were on the other side as a show of force. The lead sister—a rough, gangly, psychotic looking kid—was facing Mr. Prescription at a table in the middle of the dayroom, each backed up by their respective groups. This was insulting, as they were disrespecting us in our own unit by doing a parley in front of us and the other inmates. If we weren't already alert, we might have simply noted the cards between them as they faked dealing and playing some game.

My partner nudged me. She was on it too.

When it became apparent that I was giving up all pretense of paying attention to his nonsense, the Weasel got a bit louder and more eager to run interference. I saw the lead sister say something and go silent. Mr. Prescription grinned, nodded, and got up. They were oblivious to us, focusing on consummating the deal.

Unnecessarily, I got a kick from my partner. This was it.

I watched the drug dealer enter the bathroom to my right. A scrawny punk inmate rose and walked in after him. So that's his current mule, I noted. I gave them a few seconds to hand off the contraband, then rose and began walking toward the bathroom.

Mr. Prescription emerged from the bathroom and opened his eyes wide when he saw me walking toward him with focus. He turned before I could say or do anything and darted into a stall. All I saw was a fluid motion as he pitched the drugs and flushed them, moving so quick he practically dove into the toilet, his right leg lifting into the air for balance.

He emerged, grinning at me.

But I didn't bite. I simply walked past him and continued on as if I was conducting a routine tier check. I heard a suppressed angry murmur from the Sisterhood side of the room, followed by lots of mumbling. I continued walking, attempting to appear oblivious to everything and suppressing a grin. My quick response of not acting as if anything unusual had occurred had already paid off.

When I got back to the desk, my partner, with no expression on her face, shoved a piece of paper over to me.

"That was slick."

To this day, I don't know how big a loss the dealer suffered, and I'm not sure what exactly was pitched, although I heard a rumor about heroin. I do know that the inmates put out word that he ditched his load for no reason, although it was actually a good call on his part. They said he panicked and that I'd only been doing a tier check. He knew the truth as well as I did.

A few days after the incident, one of the Sisters got really upset when I found some unsafe Whiteout in one of the porter closets and confiscated it. Sniffing such chemicals was probably a tremendous step down from what he'd anticipated. He'd probably been pumped up about his high and found a loathsome substitute, only to lose that as well.

Turns out more than a few inmates were upset because some of the botched deal was on credit. After a few weeks, Mr. Prescription looked like he needed one written for himself. He came out of his room one night to face me, looking very worn and nervous. He'd lost weight because he'd been skipping most mainlines, feeling safer in his room. He didn't dare go to the gym or the yard, so his muscles, unfed and unworked, had begun to atrophy.

"You didn't have to do it that way. It was wrong. You could have pat searched me." He stared at me as if I was supposed to give him sympathy. I really wanted to say, "Oh, I'm sorry. Did I fuck up your drug deal?" in my best Samuel L. Jackson voice, but I didn't have one, and Samuel was still up and coming then.

"You want to PC?" I asked, offering the protective custody option.

"Why you going to act as if you have no idea what happened," he complained bitterly. "I ain't scared enough to run to you."

I shrugged and continued my tier check, not knowing at the time that when he finally got out of the facility he would be bone skinny and skittish. He survived, but Mr. Prescription was dead.

MR. QUIRKY

One offender I will never forget was a guy I'll call Mr. Quirky because his odd behavior made him stand out among a seething mass of regular inmates, abnormal offenders, dings, and total psychos. Either his survival adaptation techniques eventually took over and he became a good case study for how inmates dealt with stress, or he was squirrel bait before he got into the system. Either way I benefited, because Mr. Quirky was a trip to watch and a pleasure to have in the unit, just like anything else that made the time go by faster.

At first I didn't notice the scrawny guy in his forties, even though he was a career criminal and primarily a violent one, too. I had other concerns. There was the six foot, 230 pounds of anger management problem in the adjoining cell who recently said, "You're cool with me . . . *now*." I also had a group of young gangbangers and keyed-up skinheads that formed my crew of porters at the time who suddenly discovered family-like unity after I twice sent them all back to scrub the urinals to get out hard water stains.

Mr. Quirky weighed maybe a buck and a quarter and stood under five and a half feet tall, so he wasn't much of a physical threat. (Yeah, I know: we're supposed to remind each other that the psycho little ones are supposedly more violent and just as dangerous, but it's the psycho *big* sons of a bitches that worry me.) His graying brown hair and perpetual five days growth of scraggle under his narrow chin indicated he was old enough to have sown his oats and probably knew how to do time, so I didn't expect much out of him. The first night Mr. Quirky came out of his room and went to work as the equivalent of a trustee in the segregation unit, I only noticed that he was quiet.

Ten minutes later, I got a call.

"Uh, Martin, what can you tell me about the guy you sent us?" asked the uncertain voice of the sergeant in the segregation unit.

"Nothing." I was irritated. *I* didn't exactly send him; he was on the call-out to go work there. The seg sergeant knew it but still held me responsible. I hesitated, as I had learned to regret the second part of such phone calls.

"Why?" I asked.

"We were doing the strip search before we let him in the admin area," responded the sergeant. "Well, he starts doing these muscle man poses. I don't think he's kidding."

"OK," I answered blandly and hung up, feeling I'd been very helpful in that exchange. OK is great to use in prison because it's both an acknowledgement of information received and hints that something might be done with it. It's precisely what they want to hear. They are happy that they successfully passed the buck, and you're happy that they shut up about it. I use OK a lot more as a sergeant then I did as an officer, and it's working out great. (I also use "No Problem" a lot, and it works like a charm too.)

A few hours later, Mr. Quirky was escorted back to the unit by a Response and Movement officer. The small inmate walked in, put his hands on his hips, and surveyed the unit as if he owned it. His eyes narrowed like Clint Eastwood's before the big gunfight, and his mouth shifted from a razor slit to a slight scowl.

Utterly unimpressed, I gestured to his paper bag full of prison delicacies in front of me. At that time, every convict who worked through the night received a sack lunch, as it was figured that they missed either breakfast or dinner to sleep. It included an oddly bright red piece of baloney in its individual slice packaging with accompanying stale or soggy bread, usually squished, and wrapped in a yards of clear plastic wrap; an abused apple; what might have been carrots (the color was close enough); the ubiquitous pint carton of milk; a handful of random condiments; and those damned bland cookies that could never pass through a human digestive system without assistance.

Mr. Quirky glared at me, then examined his bag to see if the staples across the top were intact. He then ceremoniously popped the bag open to inventory the contents, lying them out for inspection on a table. This completed, he rebagged the items.

He then boldly walked right over to the biggest, roughest looking inmate on the crew and opened that convict's lunch sack right in front of him while the other inmates watched with slack jaws, heads shaking, as the little guy looked into the bag. Satisfied he didn't get shorted, he dropped the other inmate's lunch. Mr. Quirky then swaggered away, skinny arms held as if he were built like Schwarzenegger, his little chest puffed out. He walked up the stairs and went into his room without looking back.

The inmates laughed, shrugged, and continued eating.

I figured Mr. Quirky had a sense of humor . . . until I found out he did this night after night!

A few nights later, while doing a tier check, I saw Mr. Quirky sitting at his desk, moving his head and shoulders to music. Because policy required the use of headphones, I opened the door to say something . . . and heard nothing. Mr. Quirky continued to move to music, facing away from me.

"Hey," I began. "What are you doing?"

The guy continued to move to the type of music heard only by a select few. I tried again. "Hey!"

He turned, stopped moving, then gave me a "just a second" gesture while he reached over to a matchbox in front of him. "I'll turn it down," he said too loudly. I hadn't noticed the box until he reached for it. He turned a green thumbtack and sat there, arms crossed.

"What are you doing?"

"I'm listening to my radio."

"Let me see it," I demanded. He handed it over carefully. I found myself, at 0120 hours, looking at a matchbox on which someone had pencil drawn speakers, frequency numbers, a brand name, and battery compartment. It was all very carefully done, with thumbtack knobs for volume and station changing. It dawned on me that this definitely was *not* covered at the academy during the "Inmate Property Management" class.

"You can't keep this," I told him. "It's nuisance contraband."

"It's mine."

"Got a hand receipt?"

Damned if he didn't! He whipped the form out of the near empty shoebox that held every personal item he owned and handed it to me. I checked it carefully. Some staff member had actually written out, "Matchbox radio, used, color brown," on a hand receipt. Even the serial numbers matched.

If another officer was willing to let it go and had even produced a receipt, I did not want to undermine him. Besides, the mirth factor was high among some staff, and this was almost certainly one of those cases.

Perplexed, I handed it back. "Next time, you better have headphones," I said correctionally.

I told my partner, Jason, about the radio.

"Was he on AM or FM?"

"What difference does it make?"

"Was he listening to music?" he asked impatiently.

"Yes."

"At least he's not listening to *talk* radio."

"Huh?"

"Would you rather he listens to music or *hears voices*?"

Point taken.

The next day I saw Mr. Quirky in his room, moving to the music. I opened the door and he turned, grinning. He was wearing headphones made from cigarette butts and dental floss.

I didn't ask for a receipt.

A few weeks later, I noticed Mr. Quirky was glum.

"What's wrong?"

"I had to ship out my radio."

"Why?"

"My cellie kept changing the stations."

He walked away, and I let it go without comment, which was a good thing *because Mr. Quirky was the sole occupant of that room!*

THE PEN PAL

I remember him because he worked hard for me and he never complained. I'll call him inmate Randall.

He wasn't exactly your average felon. As soon as count cleared, Randall would step out of his room, all 5'6" and 160 pounds of him, stride purposefully toward the mop closets, and go right to his custodian duties. On the nights when the other inmates wussed out, he'd pick up the slack and tackle the three- or four-man job himself. He explained to me that he worked so hard because we didn't treat him like a piece of shit and didn't show harsh judgment in the way we looked at him, and he didn't want to lose that. I assumed it was just a standard manipulation attempt.

An intelligent young man, barely in his twenties, Randall would occasionally come by the desk, usually as he swept with a dust mop, and throw out an irreverent quip or commentary on news events or a happening in the prison. My partner and I would snicker.

I watched him carefully because he worked *too* hard and because he didn't cause me or my partner any problems, although he was seen as a troublemaker by everyone else. I also watched him because I hadn't caught him doing whatever I suspected he was doing, since these guys were *always* doing something! We just didn't know what Randall was up to. In fact, he worked for me for several months and I only noted one odd thing about him, or at least I heard about it.

My partner told me that sometimes on the nights when he wasn't scheduled to work, which coincided with my nights off, Randall came out and sat in the dayroom. The dayroom was off limits to inmates who were not working, but since he'd be under supervision my partner permitted it, with the proviso that he'd be a "porter on call," a bogus status that meant he'd be allowed to sit up because we might need him to work. The shift sergeant bought it because there was some truth to it, and he was smart enough to let us run our own unit. More importantly, it gave my partner an opportunity to observe Randall and catch his game.

But nothing happened. It was as if he didn't want to be alone with his own thoughts. He chatted with the other inmates at times, but generally he wrote. Other nights he simply sat there and stared at his hands.

I learned he had a pen pal relationship with a girl living across the state when he asked where a small town was located. He showed me a picture of a pretty brown-haired girl with a warm smile. "Her name is Amy," he said proudly, happy he found someone on the outside willing to communicate with him. He was writing a book just for her because she loved mysteries, but she'd been a bit disappointed because she felt certain things were missing from those she read. He was tailoring his novel to suit her tastes.

Randall wasn't a sex offender or a drug dealer or user. He demonstrated a solid, consistent work ethic, so we knew he wasn't a thief. That pretty much left bank robber, and we reckoned he was most likely in for a violent crime because he was so often lost in thought and intensely serious.

I happened to have a discussion with him one night about his crime. He admitted to me that he'd committed a murder. A horrible murder. He'd killed someone he didn't know. He didn't know why, and it bothered him greatly, night and day. He'd laugh about something else, then he'd remember that he'd murdered someone and nothing was funny anymore. He'd think about it any time he enjoyed something as trivial as a Coke or french fry, feeling he didn't deserve even those little bits of happiness. Sleeping brought only shattering dreams.

Randall fought every waking hour to deny the effects of guilt, and he was losing. He wondered about redemption. One day he engaged me in conversation.

"If I live the rest of my life as a good person, if I spend the rest of my time helping the people who need it most and deserve it the least, the other guys, would it matter?" He looked at me hopefully. "Can someone who took a life gain atonement?"

I didn't have the answer. I just had an opinion, so I didn't voice it.

He went back to mopping. He had 57 years to find the answer himself.

A few weeks later, my partner was on vacation and I was working with a guy I'll call Officer Cartwright. He was a burly, bald guy with a powerful but humble way about him. He came into the unit in a jolly mood. It was a nasty, cold night outside, the unit was warm, and he'd had time to get a good lunch and even fill his thermos with coffee before coming in.

We joked a while, then count cleared. When Randall came out of his room, Cartwright grew silent. He watched Randall vanish into the mop closet.

"What's that inmate's name?" he asked in a low voice.

"Randall. He's in for murder."

The burly guard nodded as if in confirmation. He didn't say anything as Randall came up to the desk and signed in on his pay sheet. I didn't know the man, but I knew that Cartwright was stricken. He waited for Randall to clear the area, then said, "I need a few minutes." He walked across the unit, stepped outside into the cold, and stood silently on the landing in the wind, his back to the door.

Randall looked out the unit doors each time he went past them with the dry mop, sweeping the floor. He, too, had an odd expression on his face.

After a while, Cartwright came back to the officer's station. He didn't look toward Randall, and Randall didn't look toward him.

It wasn't until after count, during the period when the inmates were locked down, that he talked to me.

"I quit being a Reserve Deputy because of that inmate," he began.

I sat silent.

"I was a rookie when I went to a crime scene. His crime scene. There was blood all over the place, soaking the carpet. The victim was a young woman who was so battered by his kicking her that they couldn't recognize her by her dental X-rays. My God, her hair was stuck to the walls and ceiling!" His voice broke a bit. "Just past where she lay was a framed wedding picture of her—a pretty woman, smiling, happy. I could see her picture and her body at the same time. I saw it for hours."

He choked down something, then continued, gushing. "This was a random encounter. A newlywed at home alone one night. He was just a kid heading off to be processed for going in the military when his car broke down near her house. No priors. We figured he walked over to use the phone. She wasn't raped; nothing was taken. Hell, he didn't even know her. We didn't know why he killed her. This was so damn brutal! Why? I just don't know."

Later during the shift, Randall approached the desk and met Cartwright's eyes. "You're from Vincent, aren't you?"

Cartwright nodded. Randall braced himself. I guess they both did.

"We want to talk, right?" Randall stated it more than asked.

Cartwright nodded again and rose. He escorted Randall out to the landing, and they leaned on the railing. Both talked. I watched warily, with visions of Randall being thrown over the railing and falling three stories filling my mind, but the big guard was too mellow and stunned for that. They stood out there for forty minutes. I have no idea what was said, but I think they spent more time simply leaning on the railing staring into the glow of the security lights and the darkness of the sky than exchanging information.

A while later, after they had come back, Cartwright took a bite out of his sandwich. He looked down at the bread, turkey, and cheese, put down the sandwich, then wordlessly crumpled up the paper and food and threw it away. He quit the department within a week.

A few weeks later, Randall tore up his novel. He was oblivious of me as I watched him tearing up each sheet through the narrow window in his door. A growing pile of strips was already at his feet. For a long time he looked at the picture of the girl he was corresponding with. He tore that up too and tossed the scraps into his trashcan. I noticed that he'd stopped writing Amy, and another officer told me that he'd tried to hand back unopened letters from the only person that wrote him. He reportedly threw them away because he couldn't send them back, still unopened.

I think he didn't have to wait 57 years to find his answer.

Years passed. I was sitting comfortably at my desk at another facility when I noticed an incident report.

An inmate in a different facility, just one of many thousand, was found dead on the concrete floor of his cell. "Inmate Randall hadn't given any indication to staff that he was going to take his life," the report stated. At least not recently, I thought. "Next of kin notifications weren't possible, as the inmate didn't list any."

It wasn't a sense of loss or even waste I felt, and it definitely wasn't satisfaction. But I felt something powerful as I tossed the report aside.

What I felt, I just don't know.

D UNIT'S CREW

For a period of time, I worked with Frank Perales, a dedicated professional and retired U.S. Army noncom who liked handling the paperwork and completed tasks quickly and efficiently so that I was freed up to do other things.

One advantage of being imaginative is that I never get bored. With Frank handling the administrative functions and monitoring the unit, I decided that I'd begin what I grandly called my "experimentation in leadership." I'd see if the inmates working as unit janitors could be forged into a team and motivated to work without the usual threat of write-ups and sanctions of extra duty and room restriction. Pay sure wasn't an incentive: offenders at that time received a little over a quarter an hour, and they'd be working five hours or less a shift. I had to find another approach to motivate them.

The crew consisted of a mixed lot of inmates, but they were as likely or unlikely candidates as any for such an experiment. I assembled them as they came out to work and considered what I had to work with.

One inmate was a short, middle-aged white male who was already a hard worker, a con who just happened to rob banks. Aside from his habit of shoving .38 revolvers into bank tellers' faces while doing James Cagney impersonations, he was a normal working guy. If he wasn't a criminal, he'd be a salt-of-the-earth type, so I'll call him Saltine.

Waverly was a young, skinny kid who, by the age of twenty, had five years in juvenile detention and prison. He'd killed a friend—he wouldn't explain why—and it really bothered him. Although he was a killer, he was greatly influenced by those around him, which meant he generally tried to act like a tough guy and a minor troublemaker, with occasional flare-ups that ended when we pulled him aside and isolated him from his peers. We worried that he was being used as a punk bitch, but we never could prove it.

Water was an upper middle class white kid who stole sailboards from other upper middle class kids primarily because he was too lazy to work for his own. He also borrowed their sports cars when convenient for the same reason. He was a day tripper to prison, so it was still just a lark for him. He was solid enough that, despite his silver spoon upbringing, most of the other inmates let him be. The funny thing about this kid was his dreadlocks. One day when I caught him dancing around with a mop on his head, I couldn't help but think the used mop was cleaner and neater than his hair as I wrote up the urinalysis paperwork.

Chicken was a muscular black gangbanger from Los Angeles who'd gotten into a serious shooting with a rival gang member. I call him Chicken because he'd made repeated comments about missing good fried chicken when we brought some in and ate it in front of him. Chicken had been down for awhile, vented what he'd needed to vent, and had settled down for the long term.

I told the group that we were going to make the unit cleaner than any other in the facility. I told them that they were all capable of smoking every other porter crew out there, and that they'd realize benefits beyond what they'd expect once we accomplished this.

Saltine simply listened. Waverly watched for Water's reaction, then rolled his eyes and acted distracted similar to the self-proclaimed "rich, skinny white boy." Chicken grew tense enough for me to see it halfway across the room.

I'd figure Saltine would just keep doing what he did, which was work hard. The wonder twins might go with the flow. The banger, Chicken, might be the problem, but he surprised me when he spoke.

"We gonna do this, we gonna do this. If'n I gots a say, I say you get us what we need and we'll get it done."

"Right. The better you do, the less you'll have to deal with me and other staff," I responded.

"That's all we ask."

Then we went to the bathrooms and I showed them my standards. I had an apartment at the time, having just separated from my wife, and I knew that I met or exceeded these standards at home. They'd never know it, but my credibility with myself made me lead by example, so I planned to push them as hard as I pushed myself.

And it worked.

Within a few weeks, the porters were coming out ready to work, and they found efficient ways of getting things done. Whereas each bathroom was assigned to individual porters, they began working in teams. Chicken, the gangsta in his late twenties, worked with the blue collar bank robber in his forties; the wonder twins hit the other bathrooms together. They began challenging me to find dirt. One day when we were due for some kind of inspection, they pitched in and hit each bathroom as a four-man crew, working in stages.

One inmate came out and tried to chide Chicken about working hard for the Man, but he stopped him short. "I didn't do this for the Man; I am doing this for me. I'm doing this for the crew. We got pride in whatever we do."

The next day, as soon as count cleared, they came out to my desk.

"Well?" Chicken asked.

It took a second for me to realize what they were concerned about.

"The inspection. We been waiting all day," said Waverly.

"How'd it go?" asked Chicken.

The only comment I'd read was, "No deficiencies noted in the bathroom," which in Corrections is lofty praise. I turned toward them, grinning, as they waited to hear what I had to say.

"I can honestly say they passed on to me that it looked sharp; better than new." This was true. I'd seen the place new, with dust and empty boxes everywhere.

"How about the other units?"

I remembered that I'd gotten word that our unit was the only one that didn't have mop strings hanging in the drains, and water spots on the shower panels in our unit were less obvious.

"Better than any other unit!" I declared.

The inmates high-fived each other.

Shortly afterward, the crew dissolved. Saltine went back to the fed system to face a good number of years. Waverly fell in with the wrong inmates, and Water moved on. I believe he was eventually released and probably makes three times what I make now, or else he lives off a monthly stipend if he hasn't picked up something nasty from IV drug use or didn't get killed while stealing something from the wrong person. Chicken's custody level lowered, and he was sent to another unit. He tried and failed to get a porter job right off, but he told me it didn't matter. It wasn't the same.

Discussing it with Frank, we decided that if some of them had kept their records cleaner and had been in the army when it had tighter discipline, their lives would have turned out differently. They only needed some leadership, guidance, and positive peer pressure. If only they'd received it earlier in life.

A few years later, when I was departing the facility, an inmate in the corridor called to me.

"Sergeant Martin!" I walked further and saw Chicken sitting in a chair, his bucket, mop, and broom handy for a ready cleanup.

"I heard you were leaving," he said.

"That's right," I responded guardedly.

"Well, good luck."

I just nodded.

"You know what?" he continued. "I miss those days when we had everyone working together, caring about getting the job done. I never was on any team in high school. I should have. I liked that feeling, you know, being on a team. I was also pretty good playing ball."

He continued. "I should have spent my time on football rather than on the streets. I missed out on a lot. What a waste."

He was right. What a waste.

8

Female Inmates

After a series of events beyond my control landed me in a co-ed facility (yes, both men and women, all convicted felons, living in the same building), I had to learn how to deal with female inmates. I only knew enough about female inmates to decide that I wanted to avoid them like the plague. This bias came from years of watching male and female officers bail from all-female facilities, telling me horror stories about annoying habits and different treatment given to the women. I obviously had less experience speaking with those who enjoyed working with female offenders, but those who did prided themselves in their ability to communicate and in their more sophisticated techniques for handling problems with inmates.

Until this time, my one and only experience dealing with female prisoners occurred when I couldn't duck an overtime at the annex area of the large facility in which I worked. The place held a small number of female inmates, but until then I had given zero thought to dealing with them because I was trained for and wanted to stay inside a medium security unit in a male facility.

The day was almost over, and I was enjoying the prospect of making the big overtime bucks without having to even talk to a female inmate when a bigwig called me and told me that she needed a janitor in her area because there was a big spill. I checked with an officer who worked the post, got the name of a porter, then pounded the heel of my fist solidly on the door to the female dorm before entering, announcing my presence, and calling for inmate Hoople.

A small, chubby, brown-haired inmate walked forward.

"Hey, they need you in the Admin area. They got a spill that's spreading. Let's go."

"Sergeant, I first have to change my clothing, and I haven't done my face or my hair," she responded.

I sometimes grin before I go off (professional terminology alert: "go off" means to give clear and precise directions that leave absolutely no possibility of them being misunderstood, ever). My lips steadily worked toward my ears in what might be mistaken for being a smile, and my head began canting when a female officer stepped up and pulled me aside.

"Uh, sarge, let me handle this one."

"Thanks, Karen, but I am sure I can handle an inmate in this situation."

"What are you going to do?"

"I am about to get that inmate to leave this room ten seconds ago," I growled, then explained, "I am about to make it exceedingly clear to her in a direct, professional manner, with you standing by as a witness, that 'I've got to do my hair' is unacceptable. We got brass waiting, something staining some carpet, and she wants them to wait? More importantly, this is the inmate's job."

The sharp officer offered, "I thought so. Can I handle this one?" I nodded and made a sweeping "be my guest" gesture—not to be snide, but with actual relief.

Karen walked over to the phone away from the inmates and made a call. I overheard "esteem issues," "programming," and "as soon as possible" as I departed the area.

Several minutes later, the officer walked the inmate past the office. I later got a call from the bigwig thanking me for handling the situation promptly and understanding how to best handle the situation. I was utterly confused as I muttered a thanks and hung up the phone.

Karen attempted to explain to me that although female inmates were held to the same standards as male inmates, they were handled differently. When this was understood, dealing with female offenders was easier, more productive, and more in line with the rehabilitative effort. Although it went against many correctional pros' gut instincts, taking a few extra steps with female prisoners actually made for more sophisticated Corrections and produced a better result.

I retained little of what she said because I figured I'd be going back to my male unit and never, ever have to deal with female inmates and esteem issues again. But a short while later I found myself working in a co-ed correctional facility. At first I tried to rationalize my new circumstances—five out of six of the inmates in my new facility were male, and I had the shielding of some professional female officers (they scared *me*) to keep me from dealing directly with a female offender. How bad could it be?

MYTH VS. REALITY

Most Corrections employees, cops, and savvy members of the public understand the role of officers who deal with female inmates. But occasionally, people I speak with sprout dorky little grins when they imagine males working in a facility populated by women. Their perspective comes mostly from prurient fantasies or such "bad girls behind bars" movies as *Caged Heat* and *Slammer Girls*, all of which are utter nonsense. With this as their only point of reference, it's no wonder they think it's all about shower scenes, catfights in the mud, sentimental moments in the rack between two California blondes, or an inmate desperately wanting a man and falling in love with the nice officer who cares or, alternatively, a creep who will betray her. And always, there's the predation of the lustful warden, male or female. The reality is otherwise.

Reality #1: Female Inmates Can
Be Just as Gnarly as Male Inmates

Many of the women in a correctional facility aren't exactly at their best. They show the effects of physical and emotional abuse, including scarring on their faces, terrible postures, drug-use damage such as rotted teeth from meth consumption or track marks from heroin, and premature aging. They generally have histories of being victims as well as victimizing others.

The hygiene of many, but not most, female inmates is bad. On average it is better than the guys, but walking into some rooms is worse than walking into a junior high boys locker room after football practice.

Reality #2: Female Inmates
Do Provide Temptation to Male Officers

Despite the existence of broken, battered women among the prison population, another reality of corrections is that there are physically attractive women incarcerated as well, and they *are* a temptation to some male officers. Each officer has his means of dealing with this issue, just as every female officer has to deal with the same issue with male inmates.

One method is to view the inmates as "diseased, drug addicted, prostitutes" or "manipulative bitches" in order to put them in an unacceptable category in one's mind. Such a perspective is not professional or acceptable, however, because unless the officer is very disciplined, he will almost certainly treat the women accordingly if he sees them that way.

When dealing with male offenders, many female staff members take the attitude that, "He can't do anything for me," meaning he has no job, no prospects, no future, and isn't likely to have the emotional structure most women are looking for. That doesn't work for some male officers, who may have far different ideas of what a woman can do for them. For those few lacking self-discipline, most systems have versions of custodial sexual misconduct laws that make it a gross misdemeanor of felony to get too friendly with the female inmates.

A better approach is to treat them merely as inventory. They are inmates. We count them. We prevent them from hurting each other when possible. We might even hope they succeed and adapt to society when they get out. But by treating them as inventory, the average male staff member is less likely to find them any more appealing than professional female officers find male criminals, perhaps even less so since statistically far fewer male staff members get compromised in correctional environments than females.

A similar approach to avoiding temptation is to think along the lines of, "I've got a lot better on the outside." In other words, no inmate can match the special people in my social circles. Because I have a solid group of family, friends, and acquaintances outside of work, I don't need to get to know the women beyond their potential for committing crimes and causing disruption. In my mind, they are Inmates, Female, and nothing more.

Reality #3: Male and Female Inmates are Treated Differently

In big prison, we generally looked at male inmates involved in minor arguments as if we couldn't believe they couldn't resolve this themselves. (The tougher, meaner one somehow typically came out on top, which was the natural order of things.) If policy was involved we'd resolve it, but generally the answer was, "Get along or go to the hole." Usually this worked and we had peace. Sometimes they started thumping each other, got sent to segregation, and we had paperwork, but we still had peace.

Conflict resolution with female offenders is done a bit differently. After a problem is identified, each offender voices her opinion and is asked for a solution. The sergeant listens, decides on a course of action, often having to lean toward one side (the correct side), and gives the inmates clear directives.

One of my early mistakes occurred when I tried my usual methods for dealing with bickering inmates. Female offenders tended to argue over such things as whether the window should be opened three inches or six inches, how high the TV volume should be, and which visitors should be allowed in a room. I had already learned not to tell them to solve it themselves because I'd eventually be up there responding to a shouting match, but as I deftly worked toward a solution, I let slip, "I really don't care."

This was interpreted as I didn't care about their *feelings*. They all turned on me, appalled that—using their words—I "didn't give a shit" about how they felt. I instantly realized that things were better in big prison, where staff and inmates simply didn't care for each other and liked it better that way.

To be effective while dealing with female offenders, I had to learn to *listen* to each side, acknowledge that I understood their perspective (if reasonable), then go ahead and give the same directions I was going to give prior to the discussion. But sometimes even this modified version of my usual straightforward approach led to problems.

BEHIND PRISON WALLS

Being Played

Just as it might be hard for a female staff member to see through an act by a male inmate, the same is true for male staff and female inmates.

We had an inmate I'll call Angel because she looked like one. The girl looked too pure to be a high school cheerleader and had such an innocent guise that I wondered how a jury convicted her. But by her being there I knew I was dealing with a hardened criminal, probably a bad one if she got nailed despite her looks and demeanor.

Angel was working in the kitchen, and I was so short on staff that I was covering the area while running the shift. She came up to me, appearing to be having difficulty working herself up to say something.

Blushing, she starts this stilted request to go back to her room, a no-no for kitchen workers for various reasons, including shamming and bringing contraband back to their rooms. It's also a matter of policy, so of course inmates attempt to beat it on principle.

"Why?" I asked, head cocked cynically, arms crossed in front of me, expression one of ready disbelief. (It's worked before.)

More blushing and an embarrassed smile. "Sergeant, I tried to use this different female product and . . ."

"Bye!" I blurted, pointing up the stairs.

The next day, Angel approached again, looking equally embarrassed. But this time I had a secret weapon—a young female correctional officer I had briefed in advance on my suspicion that I got played the previous day. I told her about my gut instinct, adding my concern that the inmate might be skilled in manipulating male staff with this issue.

Before Angel could get a word out, I pointed to the officer. They moved aside to discuss things. I again saw blushing and embarrassed smiles both ways. The inmate again went up the stairs. The officer walked over.

"Well, apparently she really is embarrassed, and what she is saying makes a lot of sense," asserted the newbie officer, not adding for my benefit, I suspect, "It's happened to me." Seeing my discomfort, the officer was more than willing to give me a detailed explanation, but I demurred.

The next day, confident and proud that I now knew how to deal with the female hygiene issue, I pointed out Angel to Officer Orebaugh, an experienced, hard-bitten female officer with zero tolerance for offender game playing and less than zero tolerance for sergeants who get played. Eager to show her what a pro I was, I boasted of my successful handling of a delicate gender-related correctional issue.

She stared at me, shook her head incredulously, then pulled Angel aside and "verbally counseled" her firmly out of earshot. After being called on her manipulative behavior, I watched in amazement as Angel's demeanor and expression changed to one of a vicious, jaded, hardened criminal.

"What was all that about?" I asked Orebaugh.

"I told her that if she kept playing games using female problems, she'd be dealing with me," the officer responded. "I told her that you knew she tried to play you and that was a stupid thing for her to do."

"Hey, I didn't get played. I even had Officer Newbie check her out," I replied.

"Do you think that if an inmate was so embarrassed, so stricken with shame that she stammered, that she'd allow the same problem to happen day after day?"

Damn! I decided that it was a good time to exit the kitchen and do a facility check.

Once Angel (from our sidebar story) decided that the jig was up and her act didn't work any longer, she slipped back into her usual patterns of misbehavior. Soon she had a write-up, and I had to do the hearing. Being cautious, I asked Orebaugh for advice on how to deal with female inmates in a hearing.

"Treat them no differently than you did the male inmates at your last facility," she responded with a shrug.

We brought in Angel. She sat in the chair with her arms and legs sprawled, head cocked, and eyes narrowed, seething with defiance. She knew she was guilty; she was simply there for the process.

I figured her attitude made it easier. We went through the hearing. I listened to her side of the story. She continued to glare at me and Orebaugh. When it was over, I remembered what Orebaugh said earlier and pronounced my judgment.

"Guilty. Because of progressive discipline, this one is a reprimand and warning. Do it again and I'll *slam* you—hard! Bye!"

The inmate stared at me with large, astonished eyes.

"Bye," I repeated dismissively, "unless you have something else to say." I waved her away and turned my attention to something else. She left.

Orebaugh looked at me with the same astonishment as the inmate.

"Hey, you told me to talk to her just as I would a male inmate in big prison," I protested.

"I had no idea you talked to them that way," she replied. "I've never seen *anyone* talk to a female inmate that way! I hope she doesn't grieve you." [File a grievance.]

I guess stating that I would "slam" a female convict might not be a good thing to say and could be taken as a sexual comment. I hadn't thought of that. My direct, "You're wrong, don't do it again, I'm done," approach also might not have been the best method.

I decided right then that if I wanted to learn the kinder and gentler form of Corrections required at a lower level of security (there was no razor tape, guns, or even uniforms at our facility), not to mention how to deal with women offenders, I needed to take some interpersonal communications classes at the local college.

One attempt—a bona fide one which I felt would be right on the money ($68 of it, to be precise)—was a "Building Your Self-Esteem" class taught in a room at the local mall. I was praised by the male officers for being slick (and condemned by the female officers for being slick) for putting myself in a room with a bunch of predominantly single women with low self-esteem, and no one believed that my efforts at learning communication skills were genuine. But they were. I forced myself to sit through two of the several scheduled sessions, during which I concluded that the folks there need more help than the inmates! I bailed on my remaining classes.

I don't even remember the other class I signed up for. It involved counseling and communicating with gender differences, but because it met on

Sopranos night, I ditched it. Instead I spent hours practicing with a female friend who knew inmates and who repeatedly bopped me on the forehead and said, "No, you got sucked right in," when I screwed up our mock inmate-staff conversations. I applied what she taught me and got better.

I also conferred with my female officers and continued to ask them how to deal with situations. I learned that if you just spent some time talking to female inmates, that in itself was seen as a solution! It seemed like such a waste of time, but it was very effective. Male inmates didn't want to discuss things, they wanted it *solved*—NOW—and they sure didn't want to get into any validation conversations.

Lesson learned: If you insist on treating female inmates like male inmates, you'll be flipping burgers in a few months. Another lesson learned: If you are ever tempted to attend a "continuing education" community college class without credits, believe me, it ain't worth the tuition.

Reality #4: The Threat Level from Female Inmates is Lower than from Male Inmates

To be in prison, a female is more likely to have committed more crimes or offenses of a more serious nature than her male counterparts. Be that as it may, prison staff faces a far, far less serious risk from a female population.

In any female prison, there are some real big, tough mommas who could kick my ass, and some tough little ones too. But it's going to be one hell of a fight, unless there's that lucky first blow or slice which anyone, in any situation, might lose to. Yet the number of individuals tough enough to do real damage is far less than in a male prison, where most of the guys could give most of the guards a really rough time of it one on one, armed or unarmed, and we're heavily outnumbered to boot. The number of female inmates who can out bench press and out curl male staff members is very low, and you hear about them. (Fortunately, you can outrun most of them too!) Male offenders who can move more weight than most staff members number in the several hundreds. Finally, the number of confiscated weapons from female prisoners is always less than the number found among an equivalent number of males.

Yes, the females can be vicious and violent, but internal competition appears to be more significant to them than dealing with us. In fact, it is somewhat reassuring to know that if you were to be killed on duty, you know your murderer *will* be caught. Why? With male inmates, perhaps three in ten will turn out to be snitches without being pressed. With females, doing an investigation is a pain not because of resistance to talking but the opposite—writer's cramp or carpal tunnel syndrome or monitor blur from getting it all down. Female inmates are more than willing to cooperate with staff in order to settle scores with their rivals or for a host of other reasons.

A shank in the hands of a pissed-off 90 pound or even a flabby 240 pound female inmate can be as dangerous as one wielded by a 320 pound, weigh-pile-dominating male, but seriously, who would you rather face? Yet this raises another important point. Whenever dealing with any incarcerated criminal, the threat of violence is there. It's sometimes easy to forget this working in a lower security female facility. I still get a bit antsy when a female inmate in the kitchen has a knife, and I have to keep reminding myself and my staff where we work and who we deal with. But in the end, when it comes to the actual threat level between male and female offenders, there *is* a difference.

Lesson learned: It's harder to fight complacency among the staff in a female facility. It's harder still not to slip into it yourself. But the fact remains that the number of officers seriously injured or killed in female facilities, though hard to come by, is minimal. Statistics for staff members assaulted or killed by male inmates, found easily enough on the Internet, speak for themselves.

MALE STAFF AND SEXUAL MISCONDUCT

Just as we back up officers who deal with male offenders, we do the same when dealing with female prisoners. But it was usually for a different reason—accusations (and, unfortunately, real cases) of sexual misconduct are common when male officers are charged with overseeing female inmates. If at all possible, therefore, I had an officer stay within the immediate area whenever I talked to a specific inmate for anything longer than a quick question-and-answer exchange. When that wasn't possible, I tried to make sure I was covered by a camera. I directed my control officer to watch the other officers, and we kept tabs on each other. But even with experience and common sense, more male staff members are likely to destroy their careers being compromised by female inmates than by being physically hurt by them.

Female inmates are criminals. Manipulative and deceptive, they are individuals who have hurt and/or disappointed everyone who cared about them in their lives. A good number have used unsafe needles, and many were prostitutes, resulting in a significant number of hepatitis and AIDS cases. They are often aged beyond their years; abuse, drugs and alcohol, and stress has worn them down. Yet I've seen too many put their immediate needs and desires above their children's welfare to consider them as anything less than selfish and self-centered.

How staff members could find such individuals enticing is beyond me, but we have a name for those who become intimately involved with inmates: *sex offenders*. Any correctional officer who takes advantage of an incarcerated female inmate is a loathsome predator.

It's actually easy to avoid problems of this sort with female inmates. *You don't screw them! You don't think about screwing them! You don't become emotionally involved with any of them!* But even with the right mind-set, there are minor pitfalls to be aware of. For instance, even the most careful sensitivity to word use can backfire.

Consider this situation. Officer O'Brien, an experienced professional, approached me following count, looking slightly irritated and perplexed.

"Tom, I've got inmate Ailment lying on the floor. She says she's sick, and she's shaking and crying. I think she needs a sergeant to talk to her."

Being the sharp correctional sergeant I am, I shook myself from the post-0130 hours zombie mode and the effects of the flu medication I'd been taking and began to grasp what's going on the third time he explained the situation.

I officially acknowledged my understanding of the situation with an, "Uh, OK." He still stood there, looking at me. Damn. This time an OK wouldn't make the problem go away; he was waiting for a response. I began to wonder why I hadn't called in sick that day.

Fortunately, this wasn't an especially unusual situation. In big prison, the inmates seldom lie on the floor, and those who did were usually either dings or bleeding. On any late night in a female prison, several will be sitting on the floor, and telling one to get up isn't at all that odd.

I knew that Ailment wasn't normally a problem, but she was a bit oversensitive, and she was prone to mistaking a display of concern as personal caring—a very different and inappropriate thing, not at all what I want to convey. Emotionally, this inmate had high-maintenance needs, and we were not there to give that to her. We sure as hell didn't want her to believe that we were any more than professionally concerned for her well-being. This required some planning.

"Alright, O'Brien, here's what we're going to do. I'll go talk to her. You stand by. [Translation: You watch my ass so I don't get nailed for some bogus stuff.] Our priorities are as follows: We get her off the floor, we tell her to get back in bed, and we avoid raising this to an emergency med trip. I want to get this thing over with quickly."

I planned out what I was going to say:

"Inmate Ailment, this is Sgt. Martin. Officer O'Brien is here as well. We are concerned about your well-being, as we are with all inmates. You need to get off the floor because you are a trip hazard down there, and it would be better if you get back in your bed so you don't disturb your cellies."

When I finally got to the room, this is what I blurted:

"Inmate Ailment, I want to get you in bed as soon as possible."

Fortunately, no one caught my misstatement.

Now that I've dealt with female inmates for more than four years, you'd figure I'd have a grasp on how to address problems with them. I do. When situations like the one with Ailment arise these days, I tell my staff to "deal with it appropriately."

It works.

TYPES OF FEMALE INMATES

The predominant groupings of female inmates are different than the males in that they might not necessarily be based on racial distinctions. In fact, an interesting phenomenon among female inmates is a tendency to form "family" groups representing nuclear or traditional families, even (or perhaps especially) if the inmates never experienced the real thing. This often occurs when it's not prevented by staff or the layout of the living areas. In the past, this grouping was almost encouraged by the cottage-type facilities that put small numbers of inmates in separate units where they could act like families. Within these groups, a "father" (distinct from a "daddy") takes the normal role of protecting and overseeing, the "mother" handles the domestic aspects, and a pampered inmate, a "baby," is looked after by the other two. The felon in the baby role even begins to take on the look of a child with her selection of clothing and by putting her hair in pigtails.

Beyond these specific family groups, the breakdown of female inmate types gets more distinct. "Mother hens" are matronly, older female inmates who look out for the other girls and are often protective of them. They can vehemently oppose those who challenge them or who they see as threats to their view of how things should be. Sometimes mother hens won't consider the consequences when defending someone in their flock, but it isn't a selfless impulse—they seek control, and they will attempt to maintain it as viciously as any inmate, male or female.

"Daddies" are usually larger women, often tough looking and tough acting, who aren't all that dissimilar to cell daddies in male facilities. More frequently than not African-American, daddies look out for a specific, usually weak female inmate with tremendous self-esteem problems. Their motivation is control as well, but where mother hens don't get sexual with their charges, daddies definitely do.

Masculine but generally straight, "uncles" are cohorts of and enforcers for daddies. By definition, they don't own the girl and they don't "dip into the goodies." They back up the daddies and watch their bitches for them.

As on the outside, "prima donnas" are princesses who seek pampering and protection. They expect immediate response to their petty requests, and they will actually stare at staff members as if willing them to do the requested favor. They are quick to become upset at the way they are addressed by officers.

"Drama queens" are similar to prima donnas, but they don't have the focus and ability to carry it out as well. The drama queens are attention getters. They will come up with an ailment that can't be proven, or they will be impacted by something that doesn't directly affect them, or become too affected by something that isn't that serious.

"Bitches" are similar in status to punks in male facilities. The term denotes ownership by another inmate. When specifically filling that role, a bitch inmate is a weak inmate who is easily used and intimidated by others.

There are many types of lesbians in female facilities. "Butches" are lesbians who adopt male clothing, normally baggy jeans, loose sweat shirts or shirts with the sleeves rolled up, short hair, and baseball caps. A derogatory term for them is "bull dyke." This behavior is normally continued inside or outside of prison, but I've been informed by more experienced staff that some are merely playing a role while in prison and grow out their hair and adopt more of a female lifestyle and appearance when getting ready to leave.

"Lipstick lesbians" are women who maintain a feminine appearance but engage in lesbian activities, which may or may not be long-term relationships. As a gross generalization, these offenders are generally more attractive than butches regardless of make-up and wardrobe, but it's the use of makeup and feminine clothing and mannerisms that's supposed to define the term.

Borrowing a term from the outside, "day trippers" aren't true lesbians but generally bisexual or predominantly heterosexual women who engage in experimentation or limited lesbian encounters with or without relationships.

The term "Gumby gal" aptly describes a weak individual who, if she'd wound up with a different guy, might have been a housewife and PTA mom but instead got involved with some criminal and is serving time because she got caught up in his nefarious activities. They are similar to an owned bitch, but of more value, with traits similar to male punks.

There aren't any female cons. Almost all female inmates don't know how to do time, and almost all don't know how to do their own time. The closest equivalent in a female population are "pseudo cons." They appear to be making an honest rehabilitative effort, but they aren't cons because they don't have serious illicit activities going on the side.

9

Conversations with Killers

Many people wonder about the darkest, hardest of inmates—the murderers. What's it like to stare into the eyes of a killer and talk to him? What are they like when they aren't posturing and when their defenses are lowered? Are they vulnerable? Do they feel guilt?

As a correctional officer, I was paid to track and understand criminal behavior and to anticipate and report problems among incarcerated criminals. To do this, I communicated with inmates daily, and it enabled me to explore the darkest aspects of humanity.

It was fascinating.

"YOU CAN SPOT THEM. IT'S IN THEIR EYES."

I remember being a brand new officer, standing next to an intelligent, experienced co-worker as the population went to mainline. Hundreds of inmates walked by, getting their trays and working their way down the serving line.

He gestured toward the room full of criminals. "Which ones do you think are the violent ones?"

"The ones wearing blue," I joked, referring to us, the custody staff.

But he was serious. "Before you've been here too long, before you lose the ability by getting hardened to it, look around. Which ones are the murderers?"

I shrugged and looked at the inmates filing through, wondering whether some kind of clothing marked them, but most wore prison khaki or regular street clothes. Since I was a newbie, so new that my shirt still had package creases, many of them tried to intimidate me with menacing expressions and cocky posturing.

I considered, then discounted, the burly guy with the scarred face, tattoos, and forearms thicker than most guys' thighs, who would have made a good Hollywood extra. A black inmate with a sinister, stone-cold glance was unnerving, but I discounted him too. Instead, I noticed something that surprised me.

I saw a small guy with a neat haircut and sharply ironed clothing. Something about him.

"Him," I stated confidently, not knowing why.

"Yes, he killed a lot of people in Seattle and Alaska."

I tried again: "The old guy joking with the fat bald guy."

"He killed his best friend."

I nailed several, plus one who the officer agreed was likely a killer but was in for drug dealing. (Many months later, the inmate happened to be working for me as a porter and came close to confessing to something I more than suspected.)

Then the officer asked me how I knew. I couldn't answer. He couldn't explain it either. I just *knew*.

If I had to try to identify it, it was because their eyes showed something different. Something was either more intense or wrong in their expressions. When you look for it, it's very apparent. To be shockingly honest, it was like the difference between looking into the eyes of a human and then staring into the eyes of an animal. It's that distinct. Something is missing, or something dark has been added. I almost want to say that what is reflected in the dark parts of their eyes isn't as clear or bright, but that's too mystical.

It took a while to figure out, but I finally decided it was this: murderers see the world through filters the rest of us don't have, and that filter is somehow visible.

At this point I've probably begun to lose some skeptical readers, and this is one of those areas where striving to present reality doesn't make for easy writing. But I'll try to explain it using parallels.

The most immediate similar example I can think of is talking to a close-combat veteran. If you've ever talked to a real combat veteran who had to kill someone up close, you know the sharp difference between his eyes and words and those of a bullshitting wannabe in a bar. Once you've met the real thing, you know.

Unfortunately, World War II veterans are dying off rapidly, as are Korean War vets. (On average, fewer soldiers had to engage in this type of combat during Vietnam and Desert Storm.) Many readers might not have had the opportunity to speak to grandfathers, fathers, and uncles who fought in heated combat during these wars, so I'll provide another example.

You might have caught the subtle, reserved manner of a man or woman who has been molested or raped and has serious issues due to the trauma of the experience. The individual may attempt to hide the pain, but it's the most obvious when the person isn't aware he or she is being observed. In this case it's a loss of innocence, and though it's unlike the impression given by the eyes of a killer, it parallels the subtle distinction I am trying to pin down in writing.

Interestingly, after working in Corrections for years, the ability to spot killers diminishes. I pondered this until an officer with more than 20 years in the system explained why this was so.

"After a while, you don't worry about what they've done in the past. You become aware of which ones are currently the threat."

RAPPING WITH DEATH

"You know why I'm in here, don't you?" begins a conversation with a murderer who is unable to sleep and who found that he can't vent to his cellie because that guy will see him as weak when he reveals a vulnerable moment.

You nod. He nods.

You don't feel fear, although you are always ready to respond. You sense this is the beginning of an intense conversation. You signal your partner to see if it is a distraction, although you know it's not.

This is a man in his late forties. You've known him for two and a half years, and he's never been a problem. You know that he's up often during the night, getting a cup of hot water, walking to the bathroom, and quietly doing beadwork in his room. He is similar to a score of inmates you've seen over the years.

"Sometimes I can't sleep," he continues. He rests his hairy forearms on the edge of the officer's station, lowers his head, and stares into his cup of coffee. "I killed a man and a woman. I shot them because I thought they'd rip me off. No—they ripped me off." You know he'll continue, telling you about his feelings, about what desperate tools he uses to justify what he did, and about what he's missing out on now.

Thus begins a conversation with a murderer that the police, court officials, and maybe even the man's relatives will never experience. He is mostly talking to himself; you simply happen to be there.

Some murderers can't come to terms with their crimes, and many suffer sleep disorders. Perhaps the disorder is caused by the introspection common to anyone who suffers from it, or perhaps it's the guilt and regret, but the effect is the same. Being unable to rest, coupled with the quiet and relative privacy of a unit at night, lowers the defenses of many of these inmates. To speak with a convicted murderer or, more accurately, to listen to one speaking not so much of his crime but of his perspective of it, is to encounter the fringe of evil.

The most fascinating aspect of talking with murderers is that the discussions are as alluring as they are repelling. The German philosopher Fredrich Nietzsche is often quoted for his observation that, "When you look long into an abyss, the abyss also looks into you." During a conversation with a murderer, you'll learn as much about yourself as you will about him, and it changes you.

When I had these conversations, the information was volunteered at each murderer's pace and in his own words. When it got serious, the tone became somber. I noted a familiar "longing to be understood" expression on his face, especially around the corners of the eyes. Often, the inmate became too reflective, drifted off mentally, and simply walked away, or he became focused on an insignificant object on the desk, or stirred his coffee repeatedly as he grew silent.

I seldom spoke with an inmate who came forward and told me that he was glad he killed someone, with the exception of racially motivated and revenge (or "git back") killers. The latter two types weren't the kind of individuals who needed to vent to staff members anyway, feeding off their own hate instead. Ironically, the same hate that put them in prison sustained them while there.

Besides, speaking with amoral killers was less interesting than speaking with one-time killers. I'd had little opportunity to speak with the former, finding them less likely to be in the medium security in which I worked. They have been studied extensively anyway, and the mounds of material available about them simply distills to, "They are different than us." On the other hand, the one-time killer—the guy who murdered a friend, family member, or utter stranger who did them no harm—*knew* it was wrong when he took a life. These people are like us, but they've crossed a line.

"I don't know why I killed her." This odd comment emerges so frequently that I think some murderers don't understand their actions any more than we do. In fact, the inmates' inability to explain why a senseless killing took place disturbed one of my partners greatly. Eventually he left the department and the field of Corrections entirely.

As complex an issue as this is, below I have attempted to categorize the emotions and perspectives different incarcerated murderers have voiced about their crimes. Some inmates drifted between the categories. Very few didn't fall into one or another. But one thing was true about all of them— they never truly got past what they'd done. It was in their minds forever, and it often emerged when they would otherwise be at peace, crushing momentary happiness. LTC David Grossman stated it well in his book *On Killing*:

> *The psychological trauma of living with what one has done to one's fellow man may represent the most significant toll taken by atrocity. Those who have committed atrocity made a Faustian bargain with evil. They have sold their conscience, their future, and their peace of mind for a brief, fleeting, self-destructive advantage.*

Awed/Stunned

The slim Hispanic offender, who'd been spent more time in prison than the combined ages of me and my partner, didn't meet my eyes with his teary ones, as if he was ashamed. His mother raised him, and he'd gone to church and been an active participant in services. He'd stayed away from gangs. He'd worked since a young age. He'd had strong ethics prior to committing his felony.

Garza's voice quivered as he spoke softly.

"It was over before I knew it. It's too easy to kill someone. One minute she was alive, able to smile, to fuck, to give birth; the next she was beyond caring. She was just a pile of skin, of bones and meat, just lying there. I did that to her. From that point on, she'll only grow cold and rot. I did that to a person. We shouldn't have the power to kill someone."

Regret/Remorse

Working one night on extra duty, away from his gangbanger buddies, Johnson leaned against the counter, looking oddly young and yet old at the same time. He spoke to my partner, and I listened in, his voice soft so he'd not be overheard by the other inmates.

"I looked down and saw him just there, not even bleeding anymore. I was pissed because he was dead because I didn't mean to kill him. From that moment on, I don't have no right to be happy. When I start to laugh at something now, like what's on TV, it comes back to my mind and I stop. No more Christmas's like a kid for me anymore. I don't deserve any of that after what I did. It's not going to go away. Nothing I can do will make it better."

Denial

A Caucasian inmate in his mid thirties, White was a rugged, confident guy, but the veneer parted when he described his crime. He only broke for a moment, then went back to mopping with vigor.

"I wouldn't have done it if I hadn't been stoned. I didn't mean to kill her. I didn't want to kill her. I just wanted to scare the bitch with the gun and it went off. I'm not a bad person. I didn't intend to hurt no one. It just happened."

Rationalization

A black male with gold wire-frame glasses, generally seen with a book popped open in front of him, Green was educated but aware of his roots. He slipped away from his usual proper grammar when explaining his crime.

"He made me do it. He dissed (disrespected) me, and everyone would have gone around saying I wasn't a man if I just let it go. I didn't have a choice. He didn't give me no choice. Now I'm locked up and everyone got all teary eyed and put up his pictures when they didn't give a shit about him before."

AFTERWORD

One of the horrible parts about dealing with dangerous criminals is that anyone who lingers around them long enough and looks deep enough into their violence starts acquiring the same hardened look as them. They appear to have aged beyond their years, and they bear similar concealed scars. It becomes hard to distinguish between those who have the look because of what they've done and those who have it because of what they've been exposed to.

Hypnotic and powerful, violence is undeniably interesting, in reality as in fantasy. Our culture portrays it variously as sensual, attractive, dynamic, inevitable, and evil. But the actual experiences of violent offenders are much different than media portrayals and academic observations. There's an incredible intensity and drama in the venting of bleary eyed, remorseful killers, and rapping with them showed me how real and enduring is the price they pay.

"If I live a good life from now on, if I help people and stay out of the shit, would it matter?" one young killer asked me.

I couldn't answer that question.

THE STRUGGLE

10

Offender Manipulation

I teach a course to new correctional officers on "offender manipulation." The course covers the many ways inmates try to con staff
members and how the officers can recognize and resist their techniques. I teach awareness skills and demonstrate methods to defeat the
various inmate manipulation plays.

When it comes to officer safety, understanding this subject is one of the
most important aspects of our job, and I specifically asked for the opportunity to teach it. I quickly discovered that there existed a gulf of understanding of the criminal mind-set between myself, with years of experience in
Corrections, and newbies who came straight from the outside, who may
have had less exposure to the darker aspects of our culture.

To aptly describe the prisoner mind-set, I begin the class with a parable,
explaining for the slow ones that it is a story with a point, not a long joke
with a punch line.

*One day a scorpion wanted to cross a river, but of course, scorpions can't swim.
He walked along the riverbank, very eager to get to the other side. He finally finds a
turtle and approaches him.*

*"Dude, I know you're heading across the river. Can I catch a ride?" he asks, his
sharp little scorpion feet excitedly tapping on the gravel.*

*"No way, man," responds the turtle, "You're a scorpion. You'll sting me and I'll
be unable to swim and I'll drown."*

*"That doesn't make sense, dude. If I sting you and you drown, I drown. If you do
this favor for me, I'll be grateful and it won't cost you anything."*

The turtle shrugged and allowed the scorpion to hop on his back as he took off into the water.

Everything went well until they were about a quarter of the way out of the river, when the scorpion became entranced with the neck and head of the turtle as he swam. It swayed back and forth in front of him. It'd be so easy to nail the turtle, he thought. The target moved back and forth, and the scorpion's stinger started itching and twitching and swaying in unison to the moving neck. He realized that if he hit the turtle before they hit the other bank, he'd die. But the urge was too powerful.

Finally, before he knew it, he stung the turtle. It felt good so he did it over and over.

The turtle started freezing up as the venom took hold, and he struggled to keep going while the scorpion continued to sting him.

"What the hell are you doing, you son of a bitch?" the turtle cried. "Can't you see you're going to kill both of us?"

"I can't help being a scorpion," managed the scorpion with a shrug before they slipped under the water.

The prison-related variation goes:

The turtle complains, "Can't you see you're killing both of us?"

"Yeah," exclaims the scorpion, "but I'm getting you."

After relating that tale, I tell the class, "Now you know what you're dealing with."

The point is, most inmates are like the scorpion and they can't help being a scorpion, but you don't have to be the damn turtle. The turtle did it even when he knew better. After taking my course, the newbies should know better.

Avoiding inmate manipulation is a continual struggle for correctional officers. But it is what we do.

THE OPPONENT

Anyone who believes that inmates are stupid and therefore easy to manage is foolish. Even though on average they have little self-discipline and are much less educated than staff members, it does not mean they aren't sophisticated in their attempts to manipulate. By the time I dealt with an inmate, he or she has resisted the intervention of parents, teachers, counselors, social workers, shrinks, police officers, attorneys, and judges. He or she has already seen the best and has learned their techniques, and that felon is ready to turn those techniques—as well as skills learned from drug dealers, gang members, rapists, pimps, and prostitutes—on me!

Inmates can sense a vulnerability or know how to probe for one in ways that challenge even skilled interrogators. They can be direct or slick about it, and they have "24-7 to your 8," which means they have 24 hours, seven days a week, to work on you versus your eight hours a day on the job. I've seen officers fired, get labeled a racist, lose their confidence, be charged with an offense, and become compromised because they made some mistake or did something stupid that was immediately exploited by inmates.

If an officer is skilled at resisting inmate manipulation, the cons might start working other, more vulnerable staff members against that officer. It's amazing how high up the chain an inmate can manipulate the staff, while a dedicated officer might not even get a response to his or her e-mail from the same person!

The worst label—compromised—comes from staff. A filthy word in the language of Corrections, it indicates that the officer has forgotten which side he or she is on and has been duped by the inmates beyond redemption. Examples of being compromised include bringing in drugs or weapons to an offender, having sex with an offender, putting money on the inmate's account, and getting rid of paperwork that will adversely affect a favored inmate. A compromised staff member has made a terminal career mistake and is a pariah to all in uniform.

WHY THEY DO IT

There are a huge number of reasons why offenders attempt to manipulate staff, but in a nutshell, it is about power and striving to create, develop, and use power. Disregarding attempts to gain status or kill boredom, in general there are three reasons why they do it:

* To get us to do something.
* To get us to not do something.
* General purpose, or "jus cuz."

To Get Us to Do Something

Some manipulation is undertaken in order to get objects and services the inmate can't get at all or very easily. Falling into this category are serious things like drugs, weapons, and sex with someone of the opposite gender to such mundane items as phones and chewing gum. This might also include getting privileges they might otherwise have but want on their own terms, such as going to the yard at the wrong time or being issued authorized materials when they want them rather than when they are supposed to be allocated.

To Get Us to Not Do Something.

Perhaps the most common form of manipulation, and one that's better "accepted" in a way, is when inmates connive to make sure staff members don't do their job. Although it's impossible to quantify this category because it's hard to document something *not* happening, the times that staff members turn a blind eye toward something—that is, let something happen and pretend it didn't—is probably pretty high. At times we do this because we have another issue that's a priority. Sometimes allowing certain inmates a

A Day in the Life

To provide the reader with a glimpse of what it's like to be a correctional officer, I'm going to put you in a unit so you can look over the shoulder and into the mind of a new officer. Facing the ordeal of dealing with inmate manipulation is an aspect of Corrections so essential to the job, yet so difficult, that it can scar former officers for years after they have left the profession.

Officer Karen Mitchell is in the unit, where she's going to face the inmates alone (more routine than extreme for some). Officer Mitchell, 24, a new hire and single mother, is working overtime because someone else called in sick. Her daughter is having problems holding down her formula, and for days she hasn't seen her baby for more then a few minutes between overtime shifts, travel to and from the only daycare provider willing to tolerate her work schedule, and trying to get some sleep. She just received word that her schedule will be changed again, and she's worried that she won't be able to swing the hours with her daycare. She is sure she'll lose her deposit.

Mitchell is worried about telling the shift sergeant that her baby is sick and that she wants to take her in to be checked out because she's been told that child care is a once-a-month excuse for missing an overtime. She knows that officers get in more trouble if they can't do an overtime than if they call in sick. It doesn't seem fair, but that's the way it is.

She also needs the overtime. It's necessary to pay for the hefty medical co-payments and expensive daycare, and the daycare is necessary to work, but either way, getting her daughter to the doctor just isn't going to happen today.

Her toddler son was counting on her to take him to the playground, and for the second time she promised him that today was the day. But she couldn't keep her promise because the officer who normally works this post called in sick (drunk) again, on the first sunny day in weeks. On top of all that, Officer Mitchell is not feeling too well, and she's edgy because she's been warned that a good number of dangerous inmates are under her supervision today and something is up with them.

An inmate approaches her and asks for a pass to go to the library. He's a scholarly looking guy, but he casts a dark, intelligent glance at her. To be honest, she'd like to have him out of the unit because he's cagey and manipulative, and he's got a history of being a dangerous sex offender. Meanwhile, a second inmate, another sex offender, is across the dayroom pressuring a younger one for favors. A third is openly leering at Mitchell.

She's very tired. She takes the few seconds and writes the pass simply to get rid of the first inmate quickly, handing it off without checking the call-out [schedule of inmate activities] to see if he's on it. She feels the bigger threats are the convicted sex offender who is leaning on the kid and the ding and his unblinking attention.

Officer Mitchell would like to call that nice, experienced officer in another unit for advice, but his partner today is the bitch who made up rumors about them sleeping together, and she doesn't need anymore of that! Her own partner of the day is of no help because he's been hitting on her. He's also working overtime, so she is facing sixteen hours of fending him off. She could call him on the radio because she needs help, but the last time she did he took it as a come-on and embarrassed her in front of the inmates with his attention. She noted that they backed off when he was around, but she's worried that he's trying to show them his "ownership" over her. She had never forgotten the day he was talking and laughing with inmates and they all slyly glanced over at her.

One of her inmate janitors is doing a good job of squaring away the unit. He's not much different than her older brother—a tall, lean guy who smiles a lot and occasionally shakes out his long hair and talks easily with just about everyone. There's a definite improvement in the sanitation of the bathrooms since this inmate has been on the job, and she's getting the kudos from the nice unit sergeant, who knows her from when she works overtime. The word from other female officers is the guy is okay: kind of Howdy Doody, but not a dog.

She doesn't know where anything is located in the officer's station. The unit janitor tells her where the policy manual is located as he passes by and hints that the inmate who told her that the "other officers" allow him to do his beadwork in the dayroom is full of crap. The same felon pauses as she's walking the tier and looks down at a table with four inmates from another ethnic group.

"They're the ones who generally cause the problems around here. Hell, back a few years we kept them in check before this place went soft. You know, 'old school days' in prison," he says, looking toward her for agreement.

She just nods, not really wanting to contradict him or correct him on what could be taken as racially biased comments.

As Mitchell walks by one of the bathrooms, a burly, mean-looking criminal is standing by the entrance, glaring silently at her. The janitor walks between her and the convicted killer, talking to her casually at first, telling her she's a good officer and he'd do what it takes to make her safe.

She doesn't say anything in response. She realizes the risk of manipulation, but right then it felt good to have him there. Officer Mitchell decides she'd better be even more careful around this "protective" offender.

Soon he's up at the desk, asking a few business-related questions about cleaning supplies, and Mitchell answers them correctly. The shift sergeant comes in and glares at her, making a mental note. What Mitchell can't see from her position on the opposite side of the desk is the inmate's posture. He's leaning forward, one leg crossed casually in front of another, arm resting across the high back of the officer's station, appearing more as if he's making time with a lady in a bar than a prisoner addressing an officer. The sergeant noticed instantly that she was smiling when she talked to an inmate he knows as a player and a very manipulative criminal. More importantly, she hadn't noticed the sergeant standing by the entrance of the unit for several minutes as she moved about the unit with the same inmate tagging along.

The shift sergeant is rather cold toward her when she breaks off her conversation with the inmate. For a second she wonders whether she did something wrong, and the sergeant catches her expression change from a slight smile and bright eyes when talking with the inmate to the cold concern now on her face.

"Get back to work, Wilson," he says in a level tone to the inmate, who departs instantly.

The shift sergeant immediately asks to see the unit sergeant. Officer Mitchell isn't feeling so good because of his tone. She feels as if she's done something wrong but is certain she hasn't. She's worried about what the grim sergeant will tell the nice sergeant because she's seen how sergeants and experienced officers treated another young woman who made a serious mistake. The shift sergeant met with that girl's sergeant as well right before it changed for her.

She isn't Karen to him. She isn't Mr. and Mrs. Mitchell's daughter to him. She isn't even Ricky and Amy's mom to him. He doesn't care about any of that, and she knows it. To him she is an officer, and he thinks she's going to be compromised by inmates. She's a liability.

She wonders, what's the use?

minor violation brings bigger results, or so some of us justify it to ourselves. Other times we're just lazy, or we're tired of the arguments or of not being backed by other staff members, supervisors, or the system. This form of complacency leads to other problems, but we all do it.

"Just Cuz"

Sometimes inmates manipulate staff just to see what happens. They do it because they can. It's that simple.

HOW THEY DO IT

An entire book can be written about offender manipulation, but an overview of some frequently used techniques can provide a glimpse at how the inmates take their best shots. Here are a few common scenarios, along with quick tips on how to deal with each.

Testing

All offender manipulation efforts can be seen as a form of testing. Inmates test staff for different reasons. Some do it out of a warped professional curiosity or simply out of habit. Others do it to support their various nefarious activities. If an officer is new or new to a facility, most inmates will have stereotyped him or her immediately, but they want to confirm their appraisals. Ironically, at the time when an officer has the least amount of skills, he'll face the toughest and most frequent tests.

Testing is the most serious threat to an officer's credibility with inmates. His ability to withstand the tests will determine whether the cons will decide to expend a tremendous amount of effort on manipulating him or whether they will save their moves for another duck, perhaps that slim red-headed lady cop working the yard or the Pillsbury Doughboy on swing shift.

The Stare-Down

Officer Roberts walks into a unit and is instantly aware of several inmates staring at him. One is smirking, but another has his brow furrowed and his hostility is obvious. A third inmate is acting as if he's playing the part of a gunslinger in a spaghetti western during the face-off in the street. It's unnerving, and Roberts doesn't now how to react.

A stare-down is simply a form of intimidation, a challenge. Some experienced staff members and cons lump stare-downs with the other "kid games" and dismiss this activity as beneath their concern. After a while salty staff don't even notice them, but for many it takes a while to become bored and confident to the point where dealing with glaring, immature inmates becomes commonplace.

When I teach new staff members how to deal with a stare-down, I have an exercise.

Instructor: "Stand up. Find a partner. OK, now stare at each other. Try to look intimidating."

Students: <snickering begins>

Instructor: "Does everyone feel a bit stupid?"

Students (almost in unison): "Yes!"

Instructor: "That's what inmates who engage in stare-downs are: stupid. Remember that."

The confidence of realizing that an inmate is doing something foolish helps tremendously when dealing with this activity.

On the other hand, a stare-down can become very serious if the felon is a problem inmate, i.e., very aggressive, violently opposed to authority, or mentally ill. If he gets loud and confrontational, you're likely dealing with someone who is a bit "off" and is upset because he couldn't intimidate you with a stare-down. The potential for violence is there.

If an inmate is a stalker type of sex offender, it's a very different type of stare, as many female staff members know. Female officers who win stare-downs with violent, predatory inmates may have a serious problem, because it means they failed to adopt a victim stance, which predatory inmates see as threatening or challenging. Being a victim is worse, however, and smart officers document such behavior if it escalates and keep their partner and supervisor informed.

Sharon, a former officer who moved on to another job, told me that it was incredibly unnerving to have a convicted rapist stare at her for hours. She understood procedures and documented the problem, but the thought of what this guy wanted to do to her—the realization, day after day, that he was praying for an opportunity such as a riot to get to her—got to her. While experienced officers and sergeants have techniques for getting rid of these clowns, it didn't happen in Sharon's case. She eventually decided that the man belonged in prison more than she did, so she quit.

In a way, she was right. No amount of toughness on her part would change him. Toughness on her part would have helped her, but she didn't really want to become what it would take to make it. It was her choice.

Indirect Physical Intimidation

An inmate knows precisely what he is doing when he walks directly toward a unit officer while making eye contact, shows off his "guns" and chest by crossing his arms, leans across a desk, blocks a doorway, and violates the officer's personal space. These are all simple uses of indirect physical intimidation.

On the occasions when I dealt with an individual who believed that respect could be earned through an imposing physique and the veiled threat of violence, I expected an appropriate level of unsophisticated verbal manipulation attempts to follow. He might mention an incident in which he hurt an officer ("In my last facility, some officer did some petty stuff like that. He has to eat out of a straw for life.") or say I should be worried to be locked up alone with so many dangerous felons.

An officer's personal space should be, at a minimum, twice the distance he can extend an arm while indoors, and further outside. If it is violated, an officer generally deals with it by simply stating, "Hey, you're crowding me," or an officious "Step back, please," which I don't like because I don't like to say please to any offender, especially one who is doing something wrong. Almost every inmate is very aware of the concept of personal space, and most will respect it when it is mentioned.

Here's a more subtle technique I use if an inmate is forgetting to respect my personal space but we are otherwise having a good exchange, i.e., I am giving instructions and he is comprehending and accepting them, or I am getting good information from a reliable source. I keep talking, but I give the inmate a subtle gesture indicating I want us to move in a direction, then I move five or six steps that way, with the inmate walking parallel. I then stop and turn, my hand up, my space reestablished and the verbal exchange uninterrupted. Without disrupting the conversation by reminding him too overtly that I am an officer who can order him to back off, I've communicated that I need some space. His focus remains on following my instructions or passing the information rather than realizing he's being corrected. Telling the inmate to back up or reminding him directly of your need for personal space during a good exchange is often counterproductive unless it's done with a non-hostile tone, but in any case personal space must be maintained.

A few female staff members I know said that they feel more comfortable clearly informing the inmate that he is too close because it sends a decisive message. Many inmates perceive a shorter distance of personal space as personal friendliness, which is not what a female officer wants to convey, even inadvertently. Therefore, it's always in the best interest of female officers to ensure that their personal space is well-established and maintained.

Getting to Know You

One common objective of inmates is to get to know details about custody staff. On the surface it's expected: bored people gossip, and for many, their only links to the outside world are prison employees and volunteers. However, once an inmate obtains details about a staff member, it gives him opportunities to manipulate.

Using personal information, inmates can influence vulnerable, emotional staff members. They can also blackmail less soft ones if given the opportunity. Suppose a hard-core staff member boasted to another staff member about his hell-raising days when he "used women like they wuz shit paper" but was overheard by an inmate. He might hear something like this: "You know I might just tell your boss, Ms. Brass, what you said, but I can't do that if I get to go to the yard in the next movement."

Some of us set up straw men—phony targets for inmates to shoot for—

Rationalization

- Officer Williams didn't want to get into another pissing contest with inmate Henson today. Last week when she let him go to the yard early, he quit whining about everything else and was gone. What harm could it do?
- Officer Noone decided there wouldn't be any problem if he brought in a few extra burgers for the inmates working for him. Hell, they treated him better than the officers he worked with. What harm could it do?
- Officer Willets decided that it wasn't right that inmate Jetson wasn't allowed to have her favorite perfume and cosmetics. She was a young kid who made a mistake and got herself into a bad situation. She said the cosmetics reminded her of being free. What harm could it do?

A lot of damn harm—to the officer's status among the staff and the prison population, to the other staff members who had to deal with inmates who expected similar treatment, and to the offender because he was being rewarded to play folks.

then wait to see if they take the bait. We do this by allowing ourselves to be overheard discussing something we really aren't all that interested in. I might discuss steelhead fishing with another equally disinterested officer, then estimate the amount of time it will take the listening inmate to learn a little about steelhead fishing from another prisoner and try to start a discussion with me. I'd also note how many times he tries to bring up the subject. If he tries to take it too far, I can write him up. Otherwise, now at least I know where he stands.

When I separated from my wife, damn few people knew about it. I recommend that officers do likewise and keep personal information to themselves and very close friends.

Manipulation through Comments

- "Yo, I know you an officer, but you gotta admit, that's one fine ass on that lady cop over there, uniform or no uniform."
- "Hey, I heard a good joke, it's kinda racial, but it's funny as shit."
- "The other officers let me do it."
- "You're the only officer who seems to care about people."
- "Whazzup, bro?"

Almost every statement from an inmate, whether intentionally or not, becomes a test. Even if the exchange is line-of-duty related, it might be a test to see if the officer knows his job or to see how he is going to act.

Letting inappropriate comments slide or otherwise allowing relationships with some inmates to become too familiar can lead to trouble with co-workers. An inmate may seem to be easygoing and what we call "not a problem" to one officer, but he may be known as a racist, troublemaker, or problem to other staff or during other shifts. Even if I try to be as open-minded as possible with fellow blue shirts, I know that I will never trust some officers who are too cordial with certain inmates.

Some inmates, for example, are racists. It doesn't matter if they are white, black, Hispanic, Indian, or Asian. If an officer of the same race says one of these inmates is "not a problem," he or she will be suspect among other staff who view the inmate and his racist views as very much a problem. I've seen black officers look suspiciously at a white officer who got along with an Aryan Brotherhood member, and I've seen the expression of white officers who observed a black officer being called "bro" by black gangbangers and not correct them. Officers need credibility with inmates, not friendship.

When it comes to inappropriate comments, an officer must establish proper boundaries from the start. For instance, I generally respond to comments made about female correctional officers with, "Inappropriate! That's an officer you're talking about," followed by a bit of ass chewing on how the officer deserves respect and isn't there for bullshit comments. Whether the inmate actually understood that I felt that way or he simply didn't want to hear my lecture again, he generally stopped the comment and informed his circle of cronies of my views.

One common mistake in response to inmate comments is overkill. Many officers will loudly declare that they not, for instance, a racist if they are accused of it. This immediately is seen as defensive and likely a hot button issue with the officer. In the inmate's mind, he either is a racist or is limp enough to be worried about the perception, which means he's weak and should be tested some more.

Policy Questioning

Policy questioning is a common form of manipulation. As stated previously, inmates have 24 hours a day to figure out ways to make an officer's eight-hour shift miserable. Many have lived in various detention facilities since childhood. They know the system better than our bosses, and many know how to work it as well or better than the best sergeants. Through their experience, they are able to retain every aspect of policy that is to their ben-

---

A New Twist

One of the most frequent ways black inmates attempt to manipulate white female officers is to play on racial issues, get a response that can be misinterpreted as racist, and try to apply pressure. An officer forwarded the results of one common attempt, with a twist I'd not heard before:

Inmate: "Got any black in you?"

Female officer: "No."

Inmate: "Want some?"

Female officer [shrugs as she whips out an observation report]: "No one would notice that little bit."

---

efit, yet they express complete ignorance of policy issues that have a negative impact on what they want to accomplish. (Surprise!)

As an example, an inmate may get into a policy discussion to gauge the officer's loyalty to the facility and to the administration. He can find out if there is a rift between the custody staff and management and seek to exploit it, suggesting that both the staff and the inmates are victims of an insensitive group of suits.

By asking a question about policy that requires a detailed response, the inmate may simply be seeing how long the officer is willing to let him loiter by the desk. This ploy is sometimes used by prisoners seeking the attention of female staff members with reputations for doing their job professionally. I'd tell female officers that a good check on this is to glance back quickly when you are reaching for a manual and see where his eyes are. If they are on the binder or manual you're researching, his request is likely genuine. If they are on you, he is obviously trying to play you.

When an inmate checks an officer's knowledge of policy as a test, it has to be handled correctly. If the officer blows off what may be a genuine concern or even a test that is based on a potentially genuine concern, he will be seen as someone they cannot respect. Conversely, if he is too helpful, the eagerness would be tagged as a weakness, and eagerness will be exploited just as friendliness will be.

Sometimes it's worse for women. Just as with their male counterparts, many young female correctional officers are eager to show their competence, knowing that successfully doing so will gain respect from inmates and staff. But it's important to understand that some inmates believe that a woman's attention is an invitation to a sexual encounter, and even a simple smile indicates "she wanted it" no matter what was said.

Most inmates with genuine needs don't smile when asking for assistance. They generally don't like dealing with staff, and it's somewhat degrading or irritating to them to have to rely on people they don't like as a category. More often than not, requests for help that come with a smile means it's a manipulation attempt, or "the issue is not the issue."

Unfortunately, staff plays the policy questioning game too. Some like to play certain officers who have the need to be right about everything. By simply discussing a policy, one officer can spark an argument with a dogmatic co-worker just to fire him up. He won't let it rest—he'll make phone calls to find someone who agrees with him or will dig through policy manuals to back up his position. If he finds it and it matches what he knows, he'll come back, perhaps even days later, pointing out the policy in print. The officer who started everything will shrug and ask, "You still worried about that shit?" while nudging a partner and chuckling.

If staff does it to staff, imagine where an inmate is going to run with it when he finds an officer with this trait. By knowing that this officer will follow policy to the letter, he can work it so he can get away with his illicit activities.

Policy Violations

Inmates always try to break the rules because that is what they do. It is a common form of manipulation. Here's a typical scenario:

Officer Jacobs is working in a unit. An inmate has gotten into the habit of coming out before count clears and the dayroom opens to get his hot water for coffee. Officer Jacobs knows that almost the second he'll start to correct him by stating, "Count is not yet clear; you're out of bounds," the PA will announce that count is clear. The inmate will then look at him like he's an idiot for worrying about a few seconds, and his partner may look at him as if he's a tight ass. So Jacobs lets it go.

There's a quick fix. Jacobs can call the inmate to the desk and simply tell him he's giving him a warning for being out of bounds, then document the incident in the inmate conduct report, the behavior log, or its equivalent. The offender was testing Jacobs, or he didn't give a crap about him as an authority figure. Either way, he has now learned better.

Here is another potential trap. Some inmates will only commit a violation of policy in front of a specific staff member, knowing that she'll enforce policy and do a write-up. The inmates will then complain that she's harassing them or discriminating against them. They will continue to commit the violations in front of her, hoping that one of those rare sergeants or supervisors who buys into this sort of crap will look into it. Often other offenders will join in to strengthen the charge.

Staff Coverage

Inmates frequently commit minor violations to test staff in a more serious manner. By doing minor violations of policy such as loitering and straying into an out-of-bounds area, they can gauge the staff's level of security consciousness or ability to cover that area. If they get caught, they can shrug it off and try another place. If they don't get caught after several tests, they can reasonably assume that more serious activity such as dealing, strong arming, tattooing, and sexual activity can take place there with little chance of discovery.

The difference between testing staff policy enforcement and testing area coverage is subtle, but when you catch this activity you should note in your observation or infraction report that the inmate was "testing staff coverage, which is a security concern." This is a much stronger allegation than suggesting it was simply a violation or an attempt to test policy enforcement.

Veiled Threats and Threats

Inmates of average or lower intelligence attempt to intimidate staff members and gauge their fear level through veiled threats. They may be as much interested in how we react, by expression or in words, as in actually influencing us. Although most veiled threats are not serious, it is something that must be dealt with seriously. If an inmate is permitted to threaten staff and nothing is done, you have left room for him to take things to the next level. Examples of such threats include comments like this:

The Duck-Cam

Some inmates are much more vulnerable to manipulation than we are. One inmate came up to a female officer and pointed out a friendly mallard duck that loitered around the facility. She told the officer that she'd told another inmate that we couldn't cover every part of the yard with staff and mounted cameras, so we used a trained duck with a hidden camera that walked around and followed the offenders.

Within a few hours, another inmate actually approached the officer and asked about the infamous duck-cam. The officer replied that she didn't discuss security matters with inmates, leaving her slack jawed.

- "I knew an officer like you at Folsom. He got stabbed by an inmate for being like you."
- "Not me. I think you're an alright cop, but some of these guys, they may get even if you were to write them up for something so petty."
- "I'll do it. But know this: when a man dogs a dog when that dog be down, sometimes that dog rises up on that man." (My all-time favorite.)

Deal with all threats immediately in a serious but calm and decisive manner. Tell the inmate that threatening a staff member is inappropriate. Don't get into an argument about whether you were actually threatened, and don't let the inmate weasel out of it. Then, notify your supervising officer immediately.

DEALING WITH GAMES

It's not all one-sided. I prefer to view offender manipulation as just that—the manipulation of offenders. We use dialogue, paperwork, and displays of guts to deal with inmates in the continuing struggle.

Paper Bullets

Whenever I give new officers a class, I give each of them a pen. I buy them myself by the box from Office Depot. I tell them that I believe it's so important that they begin documenting everything that I will spend my own money to have it done. If they document things properly from the beginning, they will help themselves and make my job easier. Documenting is our best defense, and it's better than pepper spray for changing inmate behavior in the long term.

Pens have power. If a sex offender has a habit of jerking off while staring directly in the face of anyone, it's worth noting, because obviously the guy's rehabilitation just isn't there. When an inmate continually gets into conflict with similar types of people, it's noteworthy. When another tries to intimidate new officers, it needs to be put on paper. In all of these cases, the documentation may be matched with his past behaviors and affect his classification, which has a bearing on his release. In the military, this type of paperwork is known as "paper bullets."

The Actor

So far in my career, I've been threatened with fifty or more lawsuits, including one that would be held under admiralty law, whatever that is. My favorite such incident occurred when a porter had just spilled filthy water on the floor and walked off to get a mop. Out of the corner of my eye, I observed an inmate lower himself to the floor to a sitting position, then slam his crutch on the floor and dramatically fall flat and start groaning.

The inmate I'd been talking to smirked and walked away, shaking his head in disgust. He'd seen it too. He'd seen that I'd seen it.

I let the man lie there for a few seconds.

"Uh," groaned our actor on the tiles. "I think I'm hurt."

I completed a log entry. Other inmates walked about, ignoring the drama queen on the floor, or else sat down at the tables in the dayroom and watched, bemused.

"Uh," the act continued. "My back."

"Palmer," I said to my porter, who was standing there holding his mop and looking dumbfounded as he stared down at the crutch bearer. "That water you spilled. Wasn't that from the overflowed toilet?"

"Yeah, but I didn't know there was a turd in it," quipped my partner, who was quicker than the porter. The unit erupted into laugher.

The inmate suddenly recovered from his spinal injury, getting to his feet damn quick.

"Oh, that wasn't a turd," my partner corrected himself.

The inmates burst into laughter again, and Mr. Gimp sure moved well enough getting to his room, barely using his crutches.

I wrote him up anyway.

One amazing reality of Corrections is that officers don't use this easy method of protecting themselves. As a group, they don't understand the value of simply writing things down and passing the information along to others in the system.

Inmates, on the other hand, understand the value and impact of paperwork, and even as they dismiss the effects, they are extremely interested in what we write. In fact, most offenders who can read can do so upside down, because they have been sitting on the wrong side of the desks of teachers, principals, shrinks, counselors, social workers, and police officers for most of their lives, with negative information about them just lying there in an open file.

Paper bullets come in many forms. Prison staff keep log entries, because a running list of events is required in all facilities. We use observation reports, which describe specific inmate behaviors that are strange or, more precisely, strange for that inmate. Depending on the system, we also have notes, memorandums, write-ups (also called infractions), disciplinary reports, charge sheets, and cases.

Infractions are written either at the discretion of officers or, in some cases, when required by policy. We frequently do them when inmates fail to follow procedures, such as arriving late to work. They are simple but effective management tools.

Memorandums are good for documenting an inmate's behavior. Like observation reports, they can sometimes have a long-term impact because if everything works right, they can become a part of the inmate's permanent record and follow him for life.

Verbal Jabs

Good verbal skills are an important part of dealing with offender manipulation on a daily basis. Ideally, we put the responsibility for their actions on them, making them realize that they have put themselves into the situation they are now in and that they have the option to correct their behavior and avoid more consequences.

Criminals thrive when people are polite and don't address their behavior. The common thing to do in the face of bad behavior is to back off or ignore it. Yet verbal confrontation over such things is essential to folks working in Corrections because our job is to correct behavior, and how can an offender's behavior be corrected if it's not addressed. This may sound obvious, but it's a hurdle for many, many people. Being direct and unconcerned about how others feel about us is a tremendous advantage to doing the job. (Being direct but not abrasive is tremendously helpful too.)

When an inmate is starting to act up and argue with staff, a simple, confident, "You're wrong," from someone with credibility can settle things. If the officer has the right personality and reputation, something a bit more creative can be used. I once heard of a disturbance being settled immediately by a sergeant who yelled, "I don't feel the *love* in this room!" Because of who he was, the inmates accepted it.

Brass Balls

Sometimes, simply confronting the inmate directly about his or her behavior is the best method for dealing with offender manipulation. If done with a hint of confident humor, it can be every effective to ask an inmate, "Wilson, do you really think you're going to play me with that?" For most folks in Corrections, the direct approach is the best tool, allowing us to blow past routine, trivial manipulation attempts without problems or paperwork.

11

Inmate Ingenuity

With grudging acceptance but not admiration, I have to admit that some inmates have shown levels of ingenuity that made me smile, chuckle, or sometimes just shake my head. Spending eight hours a night or day in a correctional environment allows for a great amount of discussion about inmate behavior and techniques. The other method for finding out how prisoners get things done is simple: I ask. Like experienced individuals in any field, cons will usually explain how they did what they did, sometimes boastfully, but usually just as conversation because it's interesting and it passes time harmlessly, which is good for both of us.

BREWING

Alcohol prohibition in prison doesn't work largely because alcohol is so easy to make. The first ingenious example of brewing that I encountered was very common—I found a plastic bottle full of a urine-colored liquid with chunks of rotting fruit in it. I knew from the stench that it contained home-brewed alcohol.

All an inmate needs to make what we call Pruno (and other facilities call Raisin Jack, Buck, Hooch, or Jungle Juice) are fruit, yeast, water, possibly sugar, a vessel, a location to ferment the mix—usually a warm place with some circulation to vent the smell—and time. One master brewer told me that it takes him from three to five days to get some product, but he was a very sophisticated producer. I learned later that his technique included two vessels, cubby holes in a pottery area, and filtering for a clear product with a great amount of kick. He used bread as the filter, favored plums over oranges, and was suspected of distilling his mix for a higher proof. He was very intoxicated when caught by staff, but despite an extensive search only a small container was found, so the assumption was his product was potent.

The ideal job for a brewer is unit janitor (also called a porter) because it gives him access to much of the unit and he becomes a mundane part of the environment as he goes about his tasks. Porters also have access to things others might not. A jug that held cleaning supplies, for example, can be used for Pruno. Inmates generally are not too careful about the effect of residue from the former contents, and alcoholics in prison don't worry about niceties such as flavor or cleanliness. More than once we discovered full jugs of suspected Pruno in former bleach bottles, which wasn't too bad, but also in wax bottles and everything but stripper containers.

Before we switched over to clear garbage bags, one common technique was to put a black bag within a liner in a trashcan. In between the actual trash bag and the false liner would be the Pruno, fermenting away in a bottle, the rotting fruit smell not unusual in the vicinity of a trashcan. When I wasn't a conducting a search, I just tipped the cans sideways, which caused the product to spill out.

An officer I worked with had a better technique. While talking to another staff member, he let his porters overhear him say that when he found Pruno he didn't confiscate or dump it; he simply pissed in the container and left it. He then gauged the response of his porters, noting that some laughed while one became very irritated. Bingo! He then knew who to watch. Pruno production in his unit stopped within days.

After transferring to a smaller facility, I learned a crafty brewing technique from another officer. I call it "fruit with punch." An inmate takes an orange or plum and uses dental floss like a cheese cutter to slice it, then drops sugar or, more likely, a pinch of yeast inside and replaces the parts. The line is impossible to see, and the fruit, although fermenting on the inside, appears perfectly fresh on the outside. Many times while in big prison, I searched rooms and smelled fermenting fruit. Although we searched the entire cell thoroughly, I only found fruit that appeared to be fresh, which I left behind. I now figure I got beat many times on the brewing fruit.

COOKING

"How the hell were you going to cook that hunk of meat?" I asked an old con after a cell search during the previous shift turned up six ounces of beef. He told me about "steak in a box."

"Ya get a steak. [Any piece of unground beef big enough to require cutting to eat and small enough to smuggle out of the kitchen qualifies as steak to inmates.] Then you take a shoe box and cut a hole in it so you can get your light bulb from the clamp-on light in there, and you line the inside of the box with foil to keep the heat in there. The foil you get in the kitchen by wrapping it around your waist under your T-shirt and shirt." Intrigued, I tried this unique cooking method myself. It works.

High in fat and easy to prepare, ramen noodles are a staple for inmates. They frequently use it as filler for burritos, mixing it with cheese, salsa, and, when possible, pilfered meat, wrapping the whole mess in a tortilla. The picante-flavored ramen, which smells like spicy, pungent body odor, is a favorite.

One inmate frequently mixed sardines with his picante ramen and ate it for breakfast. "Smells like a dead Mexican whore," bitched an old con. Of course I couldn't laugh, and I had to correct him on his derogatory comment, but the other cons snickered about it for days. I gagged every time I did a tier check and this "chef" was cooking and was glad when he got transferred.

Much of the ramen consumed in prison isn't used in the way it was intended by the folks who make it. One inmate broke up the raw ramen and, by adding reconstituted creamer and lots of sugar, had a dubious substitute for breakfast cereal. Unlike the steak in a box idea, I didn't attempt this technique at home, but this guy was happy as he crunched his breakfast down. I've overheard a female inmate discuss the same treat with an officer, so ramen as a breakfast cereal apparently isn't a solitary delicacy.

"Cooking with donuts" refers to another cell block technique. Donuts are toilet paper rolls, slightly compressed to burn slower, that are set on fire under a bunk with a sheet metal bottom, which serves as a griddle. More disgustingly, donuts are also burned under stainless steel toilets to heat the water which, in turn, heats whatever can is inside the toilet. Because inmates in most modern facilities have access to hot water pots and microwave ovens, I've only encountered donuts in training videos and through anecdotes.

Clothes irons make good mini grills, but using them this way generally requires aluminum foil as a cooking surface, and they don't heat canned items effectively. I remember seeing this technique used in the college dorm, always as a way to make grilled cheese sandwiches.

A Tylenol Tommy cooker is made from a soda can and wire from a hanger. The inmate cuts off the top of the can, which is partially filled with water and supported by a small stand made from a wire hanger. A few Tylenol pills at a time are then burned underneath like heat tablets to heat the water. This technique won't trigger smoke alarms because the burning medication doesn't generate much smoke. I had to try this one at home too. The flame isn't super hot, and it takes a good number of pills and some time, but it works! Like donuts, however, access to hot water and microwaves have made this an obsolete practice.

PHARMACEUTICAL FUN

"Rigs" can refer to tattoo guns or to hypodermics set up for heroin use. When inmates don't have access to actual syringes, they can improvise one out of an eye dropper and a piece of needle. Even guitar strings can be turned into needles.

It's possible to get heroin in one's system by means other then injection. It can be ingested through smoking and by simply rubbing it between the palms vigorously. The effect isn't as great, but there's no track marks and no risk of infection, and it's an easier technique overall. Oddly, inmate addicts prefer mainlining smack to taking it in less harmful ways.

Reportedly, a good method of hiding black tar heroin is to simply stick it on the bottom of a shoe left in the room. It appears to be something nasty that the inmate stepped in, if a staff member even bothers to look. I doubt most of us would sniff something stuck to the bottom of a prisoner's shoe.

A marijuana pipe can be made by crushing a soda can, popping a hole in a corner with a thumbtack, and using the opening as the bowl. Crushed cans seldom get a second look, and a crushed can in the trash is very likely to be missed as contraband during a room search.

Although not related to illicit substances, one regular find during searches is cigarette boxes made of wood. They are not much bigger than a pack and are intended to hold hand-rolled cigarettes, or "rollies." Some are quite elaborate, with clever slots to remove the cigarettes. It's almost a pity that we can't allow them; unless used to smuggle contraband, they are harmless, and a good amount of work goes into some of them.

BODY BEAUTIFICATION

I'd love to hold the patent for the most common tattoo gun found in facilities, as most of them are constructed the same way. (Enforcing the patent would be another matter.) One end of a piece of stock plastic, such as a toothbrush with the bristles removed, is bent to form an L. Attached to the bottom of the L on the outside, usually with medical tape or rubber bands if the inmate wants the ability to break down the device quickly, is a motor pulled from a tape player. As the motor spins, it moves a cam attached to a shaft. The shaft is an ink tube from a pen with a needle affixed to it, which is set through the body of the pen taped to the backside of the bent toothbrush. All that is needed to complete the device is a 9 volt battery and ink.

India ink used for crafts is available to inmates, and the bluish tint of a typical prison tattoo as opposed to one done on the outside, which is generally clearer and black, is apparent. One day I noticed an odd-colored turquoise tattoo on an inmate, so I had to ask. He proudly produced a plastic bowl of the exact same color from his room and explained that the ink came from pigments from an identical bowl. By melting the plastic, the tattoo artist trapped the pigment by holding a sheet of copier paper above the fumes, on which a crust the color of the ink formed. This was scraped off with a razor and mixed with baby oil, and tattoo ink was made in seconds.

When I asked about risk of infection, he explained, "I got a murder beef. Do you think I give a shit about some itching and burning? Besides," he reasoned, "even you asked me about my tat."

Another prisoner told me that he'd obtained black and red inks in the same manner from checker pieces. He claimed he only used it for drawing on paper, though.

A common way for tattoo artists to advertise their trade is to scrimshaw their tumblers [insulated mugs] and those of other inmates. Using razor blades, sewing needles, and thumbtacks, these craftsmen produce unsophisticated but acceptably drawn scratches which they fill with ink for a permanent design.

It wasn't always easy to pin a body "beautification" on a tattoo artist, but there were ways. I once used a simple ruse to trap a known tattoo artist in a unit. I called him over and asked if he'd seen the inmate escorted to seg because of his recently acquired tattoo. He said, "Yeah, but you can't pin it on me." I nodded and said loudly enough to be overheard, "I didn't think you did that one. It was horrible, and I think the guy got an infection. Dirty needle; unsteady hands."

At that point, the inmate's face reddened. "I don't care if I get popped! I kept everything clean. I always keep it clean with bleach. That was a good tat, a full ascending crane before the sun and clouds. It isn't right to say it was dirty and done wrong."

"Thanks," I said, pulling out a major infraction.

At other times their guilt was as plain as their faces. I once walked into a unit to find three slightly built, long-haired inmates standing around in very unmasculine poses talking to each other, arms folded across their slight chests.

"Who the fuck are the debutantes?" I asked the officer.

He explained that by some kind of quirk of fate, his unit was blessed by having not one but three transvestites.

Later, while doing a tier check, I stopped by a room and found one of the inmates with eye shadow and rouge. After passing this on to the unit sergeant, who eyed me with irritation for pointing out something his staff dealt with every day, I asked how the inmate obtained makeup. He informed me that Jasmine had sixty-four shades to choose from because he used crayons for the pigment, and as long as other inmates were authorized hobby items like crayons, and as long as that inmate was what he was, he'd obtain what he needed and get written up for it later. It explained the heavy and waxy appearance of the makeup. He wouldn't tell me what the felon used for the base.

Body beautification was not limited to tattoos. One night I got a call from my old partner, a young guy, recently promoted. There was a sense of marvel in his voice. I put it on the speaker phone.

"Uh, Tom. We got this inmate in seg with a cock ring."

"What's a cock ring?" asked my partner of the night.

"It's a ring that goes around a cock," I responded, guessing.

"Why would a guy have a ring on his cock?"

"Why would a guy have a ring on his cock in segregation is the question," said the sergeant on the phone. "Do you know anything about these things?"

"Why the hell would I know about cock rings?" I demanded.

"Well, you listen to that weird rock station on the radio."

My partner started nodding as if that explained everything. Anyone who strayed from country and western was apt to be into anything, even cock rings.

"Just tell him to take it off and bag it as evidence," I responded, realizing I wasn't going to persuade either of them that listening to Stone Temple Pilots, Nirvana, and Guns 'n Roses didn't make me someone who had great insight into whatever category people with cock rings fell into, no matter what their cowboy-boot-wearing, country-assed friends told them.

"Just get it from him. Find out whether it's a purpose made one or something he put together."

A long pause followed. I had almost hung up when the sergeant got back on the phone.

"I can't get it right now."

"Why not?" I asked gingerly.

"He says it can't come off right now because he's erect."

<Click>

BETTER HOMES

A tower officer called me. "You've got a fire in the fifth room from the end, 400 level!"

I ran up the stairs, looked in, and saw the room dimly lit by a red and orange bulb. The inmate had clamped his light on the back of his chair and he sat in his bunk reading, feet propped on the chair, rocking it. The impression it gave outside was close to that of a dimly flickering fire in a dark room. Turns out the inmate had colored his bulb with magic markers to dim it so he didn't disturb his cellie while he read late at night, and he'd selected red and orange because that was what was available.

One of the officers from the shift before me said that he'd found a weapon in a room, a *spear* in the making, and he was going to get an inmate dumped. I looked at his partners, who both gave me shrugs and smirks. One whispered, "We've been trying to tell him, but he still thinks he got something here."

The wicked device turned out to be several feet worth of straight sections of plastic hanger taped end to end with medical tape. Because I hadn't seen one before, I wondered whether there was some kind of lame but not so sinister use for the design. Being an experienced correctional officer with superior investigative skills, I developed a hasty strategy for securing the vital information: I walked over to the room and I asked the inmate what the damn thing was used for.

The device turned out to be an improvised TV remote. It was designed to push buttons! It worked well enough, but some dexterity was necessary to use it, not to mention having to lean way out of a top bunk. The inmate simply wanted to be comfortable.

A counselor showed me a tiny, clear plastic box that might have held mechanical pencil refills. Inside was a little bit of dirt and, incredibly, a tiny plant. It had been handed to him by a departing inmate who kept this little bit of freedom for quite some time. Somehow it had been missed during many, many searches. The mini terrarium was doing well.

Some inmates take the Mylar from potato chip containers and turn strips of it into silver baskets and frames for pictures. A good amount of work goes into them, but judging from the quantity confiscated, these things are knocked out quickly. I remember the first one I saw, a very elaborate frame, and shrugged it off, believing that somehow an inmate managed to get his hands on someone's silver frame from a desk. A sergeant got a better look at it and realized it was made from a Ruffles bag. He said, "Not bad; guy did a lot of work and took some time on this one," right before he crushed it and threw it in the trash with several others.

MAILBOXES, ETC.

One of the dayshift officers, Joe Schrum (later Sergeant Schrum), learned from a snitch that an empty strike plate in one of the bathrooms was being used to conceal and pass contraband. Another officer noted that a "flag"—a means of letting someone know that there was something in the box—existed. The signal was a box of laundry soap placed in a certain manner near the driers. I went up to investigate.

Looking at the security screw, I realized whoever was accessing what I considered to be a mailbox needed something to open it. They couldn't work it free with their fingers, a pressed-down eraser, or a fingernail file. I figured that whatever it was had to be metal, long enough to turn, and not something an inmate would want to keep on his person because it might be mistaken as a weapon.

I started looking around. The paper towel dispenser was off just a hair at the bottom, so I lifted it and was rewarded with a "clank" as a strip of metal fell out. A piece of pierced steel had been twisted in at the tip, perfectly fitting the security screw. The inmate had twisted the end up and out to form a flange for turning with his thumb. As a screwdriver, it was a superior design to the standard ones in most tool boxes because it could be spun more quickly with the thumb.

Another neat mail trick we've been warned about but have not seen is coating a stamp with Elmer's glue and letting it dry. The postmark will come off with the glue when the stamp is soaked in water, and the stamp can be reused.

"Fishing" is a technique where inmates pass items to each other by one throwing something out on the tier and the other attempting to retrieve it by throwing a weight attached to a string through the bars to snag the item. This is a dying sport because modern correctional facilities don't have bars in front of the living areas, and the inmates can simply hand things to each other. The string generally came from the loosely woven blankets prisoners were issued, and the weight consisted of anything an inmate could afford to lose.

Finally, inmates fearing they might go to segregation have a clever technique for getting tobacco to themselves that doesn't involve insertion into their body. It also works for sending mail to an inmate in segregation.

By mailing an envelope with tobacco and matches to an undeliverable address, an inmate can ensure that in four or so days he'll receive his letter back containing the contraband. There's a chance it won't be searched because it originated with him as opposed to being sent from the outside. It costs the inmate nothing to do this except for envelopes, which are generally free anyway, and a stamp. Other inmates might do this for their buddies using his name and Department of Corrections number.

Once I thought I'd stumbled onto exactly this technique when I noticed during a mail check that we had letters going out from an inmate who'd been in segregation for a while. They were dropped in the box in a unit where he hadn't been in days. I opened the mail and didn't find contraband, but I'd stumbled onto another scam—the SOBs in the unit had been sending out letters using the segregated inmate's name and number so they wouldn't get charged for the postage!

ROD AND UN-GUN CLUB

Unfortunately, or fortunately, the lower level of violence in the facilities I worked in precluded me from being involved in any zip gun confiscations. But we did encounter other interesting devices.

When someone told me that an inmate can make a bladed weapon from Styrofoam, I added, "Yeah, and a shield from a paper plate." But I soon learned how it's done.

The foam from a Styrofoam cup is either laid out in the rough shape of a shank or put in a mold made of foil. The material is set ablaze, and pieces are added as it melts and curls. Burnt Styrofoam is black and hard, and it's not difficult to see how a shank might be made from it.

The toothbrush with a razor blade melted into the handle, as occasionally depicted in old movies, does exist. I've seen several and even had one pulled on me by an inmate, although I didn't know it at the time. I've never seen or heard of a knife in a bar of soap, and I looked for years.

One of the most sinister devices I'd discovered during a search—a stem from a coffee pot—was discarded as trash. I later learned that it was to be filled with a disinfecting chemical called A-33 and used on a rapist by a budding skinhead in a jumping-in hit. The plan was for the scrawny young buck to jump the middle-aged rapist, shove the stem in his eye, and blow the chemical in the hole as he pulled it out, hoping to permanently blind him.

I found the stem and chucked it, assuming it wasn't used for anything more than deep cleaning. Foiled by my casual disarmament, the wannabe tough guy hatched another scheme with two of his buddies, witnessed by and related to me by an officer on swing shift.

Placing soda cans in a stocking cap as a makeshift bludgeon, one of the three entered the suspected rapist's cell to teach him a lesson. Good plan . . . except for one thing. The old con had spent fifteen years on the weight pile in big prison dealing with real tough guys. The attacker was an underfed eighteen-year-old kid.

A bunch of thrashing sounds alerted the officers, but they couldn't determine where the noise was coming from. Suddenly a door flew open and a wide-eyed, skinny teen emerged. Racing toward the room, the officers saw a big hand fall on the kid's shoulder and yank him back into the cell. When they finally got the two cuffed and were documenting everything, they noted a yellow liquid residue on the floor. They assumed the kid had pissed his pants until they found the ski cap with busted Mountain Dew cans inside.

During this same period, we stored cleaning supplies in some old filing cabinets. Each drawer had a stout metal rod running its length, and they were easily removed. The rods were supports and guides for wicked pieces of sheet metal that served to compress the files. I got rid of all this metal, but I am still surprised that our wannabe assassins, who had access to the files, never thought of using those items.

One night as I sat at the desk talking to my partner, an inmate walked up and slammed down a metal shank right next to my hand. He stormed off, bitching about how he hated it when these things fell out of the mop bucket when he had a job to do. This shank had a blade comparable to a KA-BAR, ground from one-eighth-inch thick steel, and was supposedly provided to the three scrawny skinheads by some hard-core inmate who got sick of watching the youngsters muck things up. They didn't want to use it; it was way out of their league. Speculation was that the shank was smuggled back from industries in a steel-toed boot. Because each inmate was pat searched and run over with a metal detector day after day, and because they moved in groups and only had a short time to get through the search, someone probably let the guy through without having him remove his shoes.

For years, I searched a certain ledge under the unit stairs because it was a nice place to secrete contraband. Night after night, I found nothing but dust. One night I found a length of plastic stock that had been sharpened in a pencil sharpener to form a point on one end and bent at the other to form a handle. This vicious device had a killing length and appeared to be of stiff enough material to do some damage. What bothered me and my partner the most was the fact that we'd just gotten a new brand of Scotch tape and opened a roll the night before. The new type of tape was wrapped around the handle. Alex checked the pencil sharpeners in the unit and didn't find any plastic residue, but they had been recently emptied. We got the impression that not only was this a recently made weapon, it was purpose built. This was a big find.

Later we learned that the shank was made for a Native American inmate who was angry with an officer. We couldn't prove it other than the snitch grams we received, but it was enough to get the offender moved out of the unit. To the eternal credit of the guts of the officer who was targeted, he refused to leave the unit when offered another post.

INMATE LIES

The ability of some inmates to instantly cough up the most outrageous excuses for their behavior, no matter how red-handed they were caught, makes for interesting listening. Whether they're bullshitting about something they've seen or trying to explain their behavior or circumstances, many inmates are just plain funny. Rather than try to describe it myself, I'll let them talk for themselves.

The Coke Coat

"When I got popped [for possession], when I fell, it was so outrageous they gonna make a case study of it. They teach new cops in cop school how they busted me. I still don't believe it an' I wuz there.

"What happened wuz I got tagged for something unrelated, I was non-resistive, thinking I was free and clear, until I got shook down by the Man. He goes through, finds nothing. He gets all red faced and says 'I know you're holding' so he shakes me down again. This time he turns my shit inside out. I'm standing there, shirt untucked, pockets flapping, socks down, shoes off, and they's about to give up, when he goes digging again in my coat pocket.

"He goes worming his fingertip in the corner and finds something with his fingertip. He empties my coat pocket so everything falls to the floor. That way they can scoop together the coke with the pocket lint and floor dust jus so there's enough to weigh.

"I gets to court and even the judge's eyebrow goes up when he hears the story. He says '1/160th of a ounce? 1/160th? What the hell is 1/160th of a ounce? You had to call NASA to measure that!'

"The prosecutor winks at the judge, the judge winks back, so I sees whaz coming. I notice the lady with glasses ain't typing. I try to bump my public pretender [defender] awake, and I say, 'You might want to hear some of this.' But they wuz done talking when he opened his eyes. The judge drops the hammer, and it's over.

"Then I remembers my coat was sewed together in Colombia! Down there they got so much coke it's floating in the air. Some just had to wind up in the pocket.

"But it came out too late, so here I am."

I didn't think anyone would top that, but a female inmate did:

For the Birds

"I was on the corner, talking wi' my girls when County pulls up and says I'm dealing.

"Next thing I know I'm all bent up over the hood of the Crown Vic with cuffs on, and the cop points to somethin'. There's a speck on the bumper. He says 'Did you just spit that out?'

"I says, 'Man, that shit is *bird* shit!'

"But he takes out the kit, scrapes off the shit, and he begins testing it.

"I start thinking, 'If that bird's on crack, I'm fucked.'

"So here I am."

12

Things You Really Didn't Want to Know About Corrections

Whether you're involved in Corrections or simply purchased this book out of morbid curiosity, this is the chapter you'll dog-ear and share with your friends. If you're sensitive, this chapter will stun you and possibly cause you to put this book down for good. Make sure that it's been a while since you've eaten, because some of this material is rough.

This friendly opening advice isn't offered for shock value; it's given because I need to get across the fact that prison ain't no joke. The following material relates to the behavior of some of the worst inmates and includes the practices of pedophiles, rapists, murderers, and the mentally ill.

You picked up this book wanting reality.

Well, here it is.

AN INTRODUCTORY STORY

Working in Corrections changes people, and some of that change isn't for the good. While working in prisons, I witnessed things I never wanted to see, didn't want to comprehend, and wish I could forget. To avoid embarrassing myself, and to prevent exposure through ignorance to substances best left for clean up, I continually queried officers, nurses, and inmates on various subjects to expand my knowledge beyond my personal observations and experiences.

People working in prisons necessarily have gritty senses of humor; it helps us deal with some pretty grim aspects of life. I'll break you in on this chapter the same way I begin teaching a fresh officer, with a story taught to many newbies (including me) at the academy. It's about an incident I was glad didn't happen to me.

On day one, I showed up in my immaculate uniform, with creases you could cut a steak with. My shoes and badge were highly polished, and I was clear-eyed and ready to work. I strode up to the sergeant in the old cell house and announced my presence. He didn't even look up from his newspaper. "Get your ass up on the tier and help 'em shake it down," he growled.

I figured this would be my time to shine. I marched right up and began searching. This was back before "universal precautions"—the prissy guys were the ones who washed their hands after doing the searches, and latex gloves and masks just weren't available.

I was going through the cells without finding anything significant when I stumbled upon something that I just knew had to be important. It was well hidden, wrapped in a dirty shirt and secreted beneath a mattress. It was made of plastic, very heavy, and unlike anything I'd seen before.

Although it was too short for a club, I figured it was some kind of weapon. I picked it up and showed it to the other officers. It had to be a good find. They laughed and congratulated me. One old-timer told me to rush it down and show the sarge right away!

I took the item down to the sergeant. He looked up, leaned back, and grinned at me. He asked me if I knew what the object was. I admitted I didn't. He instructed me to take the contraband to the lieutenant immediately and plop it down on his desk to impress him.

I went right down to the LT's office and walked in. He was signing some papers. I put the object on his desk and it rolled down to his hand holding the pen. He stared at the item, then glared up at me.

For the next ten minutes, the LT explained in graphic detail what a dildo was and what I could do with the next one I found.

This was my first day.

Like the newly educated officer in the story, I want to avoid being embarrassed or infected by something I stumble upon while doing my job. What shocks me is that so many of my peers never learn about the disgusting and disturbing things that occur around them daily in big prison. Some officers are so naïve that they remain clueless, while many are in denial. A few are too stupid to care. Sometimes I wished I wasn't as observant, that I didn't listen as well as I did, and that I'd forget some of the things I learned, but in the end it is better to know about them so you can recognize and avoid them.

Remember that most inmates eventually go back out into society and continue these behaviors. Perhaps everyone should know what criminals are capable of and face the fact that what is sometimes considered an "urban myth" or sickening horror story is actually reality.

WHY WE WEAR GLOVES

Plungers, mop handles, and brooms are frequently found in the showers of an adult facility, providing there are individual stalls. These items are brought in by male inmates to anally gratify themselves. I've had the distasteful task of telling officers who griped about finding such objects in the showers not to touch them without gloves. Unfortunately, the officer was often holding the stained tip of the length of wood in his hand while I enlightened him.

Pens are used by inmates in the same manner, so I advise officers to bring their own pens and not to trust the ones in the desks since other staff might have snagged them in a room search and tossed them in the drawer without checking. One officer couldn't get a pen to write, so he disassembled it and found out what filled it—feces. Now he brings his own pens.

I saw a poster in a tavern bathroom that warned that less than 65 percent of people washed their hands after using the bathroom, and less than half of them used soap! The ratio for inmates must be just as bad, but I've seen officers lend their pens to inmates, then watched them absentmindedly *chew* the same pens after they were returned. I usually kept one pen to hand to inmates, another to lend to staff members, and one for myself. I have even cleaned pens with waterless sanitizer after letting inmates use them.

One convicted rapist confided in me that I should keep my hands off the railings on the tiers when I worked with female officers in the unit, especially the "fine ones." He told me that someone—not him, of course—but *someone* in the unit would masturbate in his room, come out and smear semen on the railings, and wait to see if the female officers touched the railing, getting all happy when they did. When I thought about it, I *had* felt various wet and gritty things on the railings in the past.

This criminal also informed me that out on the streets, some offenders did the same thing with money. They handed these filthy dollars to fine-looking waitresses, female employees at fast-food places, clerks in stores,

---

Now There's Something You Don't See Everyday

One officer reportedly caught a pair of inmates engaged in sexual activity. Because of the cramped location (a toilet stall) and the activity (you don't want to know), the officer found the inmates in a very, very strange pose, made even more surreal from his view, which came from popping his head over the top of the stall and looking straight down. In addition to what they were doing to each other, they had brought other items along for the fun. Let's just say these were some very active fellows who covered all the bases.

"How the fuck am I gonna document this one?" asked the discovering officer over and over, shaking his head as he considered each item.

"In detail," replied the humorless sergeant. "It's gotta stick."

Ironically, the officer caught the pair because of sticks. He'd been looking for a plunger for a clogged toilet when he happened upon the stall and found the handles of the plungers already in use.

When questioning the inmates as to what the hell they were thinking, one said that he was merely getting his Christmas present early.

It was late August.

---

and, of course, topless dancers. They also smeared their semen on pay phone mouthpieces, escalator railings, elevator buttons, and water fountain splash guards—anywhere a person was likely to touch a surface without thinking. It's a whole perverted game of smearing semen and not getting caught, then getting one's jollies either watching a woman (or a child) touch the nasty stuff or simply knowing it's happening. And people actually come down on us for incarcerating these "unfortunates."

Men aren't safe because of the random nature of this practice; sometimes they are actually targeted. One inmate told me that in the army they caught a homosexual soldier doing the same thing with other guy's canteens and other gear.

While conducting room searches, officers have to watch out for washcloths, T-shirts, and single socks tucked under mattresses since they are frequently "shot rags"—cloths used to catch ejaculate. I once requested and got permission to dump an inmate because he threw a shot rag into his cell mate's face. His cellie was getting out the next day, and the jealous inmate wanted to provoke him to fight so he would lose good time and get caught up in the system for a while. To his credit, the targeted inmate avoided fighting by leaving the room, wrapping his hands around the railing, and staring at a photo of his girlfriend. She'd been faithful, he explained, waiting for him to come out for several years. If he hadn't felt he owed the girl, he'd have torn the pervert apart.

If an offender did this to a guy who had helped him out and shared what he had over the years, imagine what this sick puppy did to officers given a chance. And remember, guys like this work in prison kitchens. They get out and work in restaurants. They work in canneries, bars, and fast-food places too.

More than once, we have had new inmates complain that their pillow had an odd hole along a seam. The first time I encountered this, I assumed that we ought to search it for contraband. An experienced sergeant nixed the search and told the inmate that he'd inherited a "girlfriend" along with the room and that he'd get him a new pillow.

Given the environment, it's a wonder that more officers don't develop a latex fetish and want to cover themselves from head to foot with it. That microthin barrier is wonderful, and providing they're not ripped or pierced, gloves allow us to almost unflinchingly go about our tasks. Not surprisingly, and for a very different reasons, inmates have an odd fondness for latex too.

INMATE FUN WITH LATEX GLOVES

I am sure that the marketing personnel at Dupont have never dreamed of the uses for gloves that inmates have come up with. They are used to catch shots of semen, or they are blown up, the thumbs inverted (pinkies by the less fortunate), and used as makeshift vaginas. Some guys fill the glove with warm water first. Homosexual inmates sometimes fill the fingers with ejaculate, tie them off at the end, and send them as gifts to each other. (Imagine having this little baggie bounce out of an envelope during a mail check, land on the desk, and jiggle.) If they think they're going to segregation, inmates also smuggle tobacco, rolling papers, strikers, and a few matches by securing the items in a mini bundle, inserting it all into a glove finger, then keestering it in their rectum.

I've only heard about the following use of gloves from one officer who worked in a woman's correctional facility, but over time I was able to confirm it. It seems that female inmates have an interesting use for heavier gloves made of thicker material. (The heavy blue ones are preferred.) They call these devices "Smurfs."

It seems that certain "studs" go around a female facility with a device made from the finger of a thick-sided rubber glove stuffed with sanitary napkins (variation: starch-soaked tampons) in the shape of a penis. Some are even made to order, with size and shape options no less! Negotiated services with the strap-on can include preferred positions and special treatment (stroked hair, a reach around, etc.).

Although not glove related, similarly used devices like dildos—real ones and prison shop versions—pop up unexpectedly at times. It's an embarrassing moment for an inmate when one accidentally falls out of a sleeve or pocket. One officer swears he found a hand-crafted device that was not only motorized but had variable speed.

In some female correctional facilities, the larger hot dogs are used for sexual gratification. I've never heard of a reliable "fun with fruit" story with female inmates, but cons have told me that some male inmates bugger melons and even oranges.

MORE INMATE FUN WITH BODY FLUIDS

Politically incorrect or not, I emphatically state that male inmate homosexual behavior causes some of the most disgusting aspects of Corrections for prison staff, and exposure to the residue of an encounter can leave you physically ill. (No official manual or instructor at an academy will tell you that!) I already covered the "gifts" sent in latex glove fingers between male homosexuals, but it gets far worse.

One of the most common ways to catch punking [anal sex] is to walk along the tier using not just your eyes and ears but your nose. You can smell the activity long before you see it. It's a nasty, gamey, shit stench, but very different from regular feces, and it's so ripe and foul that you have no doubt what's occurring. It's the smell of shit that isn't ready to actually be shit coming out.

Officers should never brush their shoulder or lean their back against any wall in anything like a janitorial closet, because that's where the punker wipes off his fingers after scooping shit off his penis. A unit janitor told me that we don't often see it because the smarter punks will clean up the evidence or bring something like a towel along, which we later find thrown in the corner or in a bucket. Sometimes janitors get pissed, but they silently clean it up without bitching because they don't want to be labeled a snitch. But despite the Convict Code, no con is going to let something like this go without bitching about it.

My introduction to this spectacle came when a unit janitor called out, "Hey officer, check out this shit!" I learned to have them simply tell me about it after they cleaned it up so I could simply report, "Unit Janitor reported fecal matter smeared on walls. Area cleaned."

Occasionally, an inmate who is so heavily used as a voluntary punk actually wipes out his sphincter, i.e., the guy has become so loose that he has to wear adult diapers until the muscles have retightened enough to have retention. It is a test of professionalism dealing with the stench as an inmate who allowed this to happen to him turns in his diapers for the bio bin. The staff generally have to bite their tongues and accept it as a price of doing business, but we are human. In this case, exposure doesn't breed tolerance; it breeds disgust.

Some inmates, both straight and homosexual, seal envelopes with semen. We scan outgoing mail, and this practice is sometimes mentioned in the text of the letter. I doubt that many officers use gloves when dealing with inmate mail. I know the postal service people on the outside don't.

We occasionally find a container full of urine during a cell search. From our best guess, the urine is saved for its uric acid content, which is thought will kill pathogens on the penis or in the anus following sex. This isn't as farfetched as it seems, since the British Army once used this practice to prevent venereal disease prior to the introduction of penicillin, or so I was told during a field sanitation/hygiene class as a Marine private many years ago. The urine might also be stored because the inmate has taken or is soon going to take some narcotics. If a staff member is sloppy when conducting his urinalysis, the inmate can introduce the trace-free piss into the sample cup.

Using urine for acts of revenge occurs too. I've caught inmates mopping the floor after peeing in the bucket, generally after being told to redo an area. Another nasty example of a "git back" occurred when a con found that someone had jumped the line for the clothes dryer. He pissed in the dryer full of the offender's stuff and set it on high.

Saliva in a cup is another occasional find. During searches, the spit is often mistaken for water or simply missed when kept in a denture container. It is gathered from days of spitting. In both instances when I observed this behavior, the inmates were elderly, demented (beyond the usual) pedophiles. I eventually discovered why they kept cups of spit in their room—they used the saliva to pour over their penis to simulate receiving oral sex during masturbation.

Female officers frequently catch male offenders masturbating while staring straight at them. If she does nothing, the inmate will be encouraged to continue or worse, using warped criminal logic, assume she enjoyed the show. If she writes up the incident, many correctional pros will view it as an overreaction. They believe it's just another aspect of the job and might suggest that she "grow up" or become hardened to the behavior. This pervasive view couldn't be more wrong. An inmate with a history of sex offenses who continues to act in an inappropriate manner must be documented.

Women staff members have a variety of means to deal with this problem. Some experienced officers will stop, glance at the inmate's activity quizzically or with astonishment, then look at their own pinkie as if doing a size comparison, shake their heads disdainfully, and continue their checks without a word. It seems to work, but I'd not recommend it because it might irk an extremely dangerous or mentally disturbed offender into action.

After boasting to a former officer that I'd probably heard or seen everything, I received a correction. He told me of an inmate in segregation who started to masturbate, and to really get off, he decided to insert the stem of his eyeglasses into his penis and jerk it out at the point of orgasm. Well, he did, but his careless technique damaged veins on the inside of his penis, and he started spewing blood as well as semen.

A "prison milkshake" is a combination of urine and feces in a container, shaken to a more or less chunky consistency. This substance is then doused (or "dashed") on a staff member, usually through the bars or cuff port since this occurs most frequently when an inmate has been locked down. An officer working in a prison in a southern state told me that he heard the fluid called "Yoo Hoo," and not only because it resembles the color of the popular drink. It also refers to the inmate's call to the staff member with a bona fide request before dashing him.

A projectile variation involves rolling tiny balls of crap and flicking them at staff members. Inmates reportedly also flick snot balls into staff members' food and drink if given the opportunity or if they have a particular grudge against one of them. Reports of more harmful substances such as bleach being found in the drinks of officers isn't uncommon either.

At some time in the history of every correctional facility, an inmate has been caught putting urine, blood, feces, or semen in the food. This is not an urban myth. Especially favored are the wet foods, such as soup, chili, and stew. Other inmates use raw meat, especially liver, for gratification. I strongly recommend not eating anything in a facility unless the preparation is observed by someone you trust or it comes directly out of a box or can. Better yet, pack a lunch.

PAINTERS AND PICASSOS

In a special category are the mentally disturbed inmates who, for some reason, feel compelled to write and/or draw on the walls with excrement.

Often these artists begin by stripping down and smearing shit on themselves, then on the walls. "We got another damn Picasso in seg today," is not what you want to hear when you get on duty.

I once had to assist in pulling a very demented inmate from a seg cell that he had decorated with some statement in 7 inch lettering. Oddly enough, his "handwriting" was quite neat, and he used the rows of cinderblock like lined notebook paper. What he wrote didn't matter, but it had something to do with his take on the Bible. He had done this with a mind that was totally gone and with eyes that didn't register on us, on the nurse, or on anything.

It was a disturbing and intense experience. Although we were thoroughly annoyed and disgusted, I noticed that my fellow officers, all experienced hard-core old timers, treated the inmate in a professional manner and with neutral expressions despite their revulsion. We maintained minimal conversation, and the only sounds were the crackle of our radios and the muffled laughter of the insane inmate, a huge black guy with a shaved head, wrapped in a sheet, rocking back and forth on his bunk as he watched us. The experience was somber and stark—it's horrible to see someone whose mind has decayed to that point.

CREEPY CRAWLIES

I'm going to make the gross assumption that the average reader already knows about head lice, as kids will be kids and share combs and hats, but you might not know about public lice, also known as crabs or scabies, which are actually mites.

Mites live everywhere, including on us, and we probably ingest millions in a lifetime on our butter, cheese, and other foods. But mites do a bit of payback—they use us for toilets. The itching, redness, and swelling at the joints they cause is due to their burying waste under our skin. They are nasty little creatures.

Recently, I informed my officers that one of the rooms was infested with pubic lice. With a serious expression, Officer O'Brien stated, "Infract them."

"What would you write them up for?" someone asked.

"Unauthorized pets," he dead panned.

"No, unauthorized visitors," I tossed in. "Vermin on vermin."

Another time, a porter called out to me and said, "You gotta see this." He was in the lower bathroom pointing to the top of a urinal. I walked over, looked, and didn't see anything.

"Here, watch this," he stated, putting his finger down on the cold porcelain.

I then noticed small specks of off-white with miniscule reddish centers. The things started *moving*. The inmate pulled back his finger just in time.

"Some sick bastard must have picked them off and left them here.

It's Not Only Prisoners

My supervisor told me that we had a punk kid, a street hustler in the unit who was being leaned on by an older con. The kid wanted to do straight time and not be pressured. We "persuaded" the older guy to lay off, letting him know that we were all going to let the kid do his time and have his space. The con, being a true con, backed off and sought some way to kill time.

The former punk approached us and provided some interesting info that I initially dismissed. (Punks are often weak all around, including in their roles as snitches.) He claimed he'd serviced some local luminaries, big names from the big city, when he was a youngster. I assumed he was full of crap; I respected some of the guys he named, and they were municipal leaders. I didn't want to believe him.

Over the years, however, one of the guys he named was arrested for sexual misconduct with a young teen, using an approach that matched what the punk had described. Another was proven in court to be a child molester. A third was strongly supported for a government position by yet another child molester the punk had identified. (Pedophiles sometimes work in rings and are tight with each other.) I am still waiting for them to be exposed.

They're still alive," he explained unnecessarily.

The bathroom was infested. I looked about the otherwise clean place and uttered the first thought that came to mind.

"Close it off. I want this placed bleached out, top to bottom. I want those nasty things dead. I want their next generation dead. I want to know that not even their dried-out shells exist."

This incident reminded me of a discussion with an old con. The dirtiest thing he'd ever seen was when some of inmates would cap one end of a Bic pen tube, fill it with crabs, and plug the other end. They'd then walk behind some officer or inmate they especially disliked and pea shoot the critters onto his back, taking bets on how long it would be until they saw him start scratching.

PORNOGRAPHIC MAGAZINES AND PHOTOS

Why pornographic magazines aren't banned in correctional facilities is beyond me. In an environment where a dirty joke can get a staff member nailed for sexual harassment, incarcerated sex offenders are permitted to have porn. This includes guys who *killed* their victims!

A female officer once told me that one of the most degrading aspects of her job was being forced to hand deliver to the inmates their *Penthouse* and *Playboy* magazines while they leered at her. Imagine the problem she faces when inmates find a pictorial, especially a raunchy one, that displays a model who looks similar to her. Many inmates will want to believe it is her; others will look at the pictures and visualize that it is her. They might even mention the pictorial to a weak male staff member and try to get rumors started about the female officer's past. In all of these cases, the officer's credibility is eroded.

Inmates display photos of beautiful women in order to manipulate female officers as well, making such comments as, "She only wants the pics down because she wishes she looked that good" when the officer deals with the contraband, or "Damn, that female cop was looking really hard at them pictures," implying that the officer was turned on by the photos when she was simply checking to see if they exceeded obscenity standards. Race-baiting African-American inmates take it a step further, noting the majority of white women who appear in pornography magazines and saying things like, "You don't see the sisters doing that as often."

But commercial pornography wasn't the only problem. While conducting searches, we were supposed to go through the shoe boxes full of photos we found because they sometimes revealed such evidence as gang signs, tattoos, weapons, and, most shockingly (and, fortunately, extremely infrequently), images of female staff members (some get stupid and compromised). Yet in these stashes we also found pictures of women posing in the most obscene manner for inmates. Some readers may think that officers don't mind this duty, but let me make it clear: these are truly foul images of singularly unattractive individuals.

It gets even more disturbing. When I was new, I worked in a unit with an experienced officer and observed something I considered odd. Inmate after inmate came up asking to see a catalog for a major department store. It was also a store day, when the offenders could purchase things like Coke, chips, and cigarettes from the canteen, and I happened to have a list that detailed how much money each one of them had on the books. Most of the inmates asking for access to the catalog didn't have much credit on the books, if any, so I had to ask the older officer why they wanted to see a department store catalog.

"Mostly perverts," he explained, going back to his crossword puzzle.

I stared at him, confused. "Women in bras? Big deal. They got *Penthouse*."

Giving me the "you fucking cherry" look, he shook his head and continued. "They have pictures of kids in underwear in the catalog," he explained. "That's why I asked you to flip through it each time it got returned, to make sure that none of the pages got pulled."

Well, we couldn't check the catalog every time, and eventually pages disappeared. Periodically, we'd find pictures of kids in skivvies in manila envelops under bunks. For the same reasons, many inmates have subscriptions to teen-focused magazines. And the sad part is, it's allowed.

On a related note, in college I took a class on the media, and I learned something that I seriously doubted then but confirmed while working in prison. Some womens' magazines featured inexplicable, allegedly "artistic" photos of nude children in them. Flipping through some of these glossies, you'd find questionable pictures of children that weren't exactly ads, didn't illustrate articles, and didn't seem to have any real purpose. Just pictures, usually black and white, of kids in the raw.

My professor said the purpose of those photos was to boost circulation because circulation dictated ad rates, and ads, not subscriptions, paid for the magazines. But, he claimed, most women who bought the magazines weren't interested in kid pics—they wanted to see how other women dressed and what looked good. However, some publishers realized that their magazines were purchased by males who wanted to see women looking good, in briefs or otherwise. The prof suggested that some of these publishers also knew that a good number of the magazines were purchased by pedophiles who (until the Internet) weren't able to obtain questionable photos of children openly. After finding such pictures hidden among the items belonging to sex offenders in prison, I now believe that my professor was correct.

A similar issue are the ads that suggest acts of rape and murder, most of which rely upon the expressions of the models to convey the menace. One example I saw showed a sequence of photos of a pursuit on a beach at night. One of the last shots was of a leering, scraggly looking guy standing over a lovely, terrified woman on her knees, twisting her arm. The final shot was of the girl lying on her back on the sand amid the trash, clothing askew, her head turned away from the camera (dead?), and the guy waking away smoking.

I'd like to see the folks who made that editorial decision put out in the big yard. I think they're as criminal as anyone I've counted on the tiers.

FAMILY PHOTOS

Several years ago I witnessed a disturbing incident that fired up not just the prisoners but a few officers as well. An older inmate, so angry he was shaking with rage, came into the dayroom and started screaming at his cellie, a pedophile. It took us half an hour to calm him down and learn what happened.

He'd returned from his work early and found that his roommate had pulled the picture of his child from the bulletin board and taken it to the bathroom. It was an old picture of a child who died in some kind of accident twenty years ago, and it was the only thing the guy had left of his child. The old guy said that he could no longer even look at the picture without thinking about what the other inmate had done while staring at it.

In another incident, I entered a room while preparing an inmate for a medical transport and noted several 8 x 10 photos on his bulletin board of a nude woman alone and in compromising poses with another woman. I instructed the inmate to discard the contraband since I assumed they were cut out of a magazine, but he countered that they were pictures of his wife. And as it turned out, they were!

Another criminal lent pictures of his barely teenaged daughter to other inmates and charged them store to talk sexually with her over the phone and to write hot letters and get responses. I'd like to emphasize that this was the inmate's *daughter* that he was pandering and that she was a child. Proving that this was a occurring was another matter, but the information came from a really solid source (an accurate snitch). Like so much of what takes place in prison, it's one inmate's word against another. I felt for a child I didn't know because this guy likely used her when he was on the streets and would again the second he got out. Even prison couldn't stop him.

Considering the fact that the inmates know that their cellie is a fellow criminal and that his background might include sex offenses and violence, it's amazing that they post pictures of children, girlfriends, and wives on their bulletin boards in their rooms. Any passing offender can see them as well, and some of them will be back on the streets long before the dork who posted the photos. These departing inmates now know exactly what the other prisoner's family members look like. They might also have discovered their addresses, phone numbers, nicknames, and habits as well as what schools the children attend, where the wife works, and even which hours the children are not under adult supervision. Yet despite this obvious danger, foolish inmates continue to post pictures of their loved ones looking their best.

Stupid.

SOMETIMES YOU HAVE TO JUST LET IT GO

Inmates frequently let us know that they have serious or incurable diseases, whether as a ploy for sympathy or to appear more threatening. In the criminal mind, anything can be used as leverage. Officers aren't supposed to divulge this information to anyone no matter what because of an inane interpretation of a prisoner's right to privacy. This hobgoblin of inmate privacy involves serious liability issues and constitutional rights, so we respect it.

We'll proceed with a hypothetical (and composite) example:

As a unit officer, you find out that an inmate has "caught death"—he has Acquired Immune Deficiency Syndrome, AIDS. He tells you this, and you know he isn't lying because of the medications he takes. He knows he is going to die eventually, and he doesn't care who he infects. You suspect he's boffing his cellie, a young kid, down for the first time, who doesn't know how to do time. He's doing what he's doing because his cell daddy keeps him high everyday, making everything go smoother. The kid doesn't have much time to serve and figures it's the best way to pull through. In other words, he ain't thinking.

You learn from an officer who works in Visiting that the kid's girlfriend is a nice girl. "Sally" is a fresh-faced teen, just out of high school. She's got a clean record, genuine blushes, the works. She's a good kid—in other words, exactly the type of person we are trying to protect in society by keeping these clowns locked up. The kid was her boyfriend back in high school, and she's stuck with him two or three years running while he's down.

You figure the odds are good that Cell Daddy gave the kid AIDS, and you figure the odds are huge that when the kid leaves prison he's gonna nail Sally, and she too is going to catch it.

You can't warn the kid. You can't warn Sally. And because you're only operating within your limitations, you can't do much except tell your supervisor what you phrase as "suspicions" or "suspected sexual activity." You damn well better not mention that you know about the guy having a disease for any other reason than the guy told you himself. The sergeant isn't permitted to call the medical staff and confirm because they aren't supposed to tell him, and he'd just be compromising them because in a case like this they would want to help the staff.

You attempt to catch Cell Daddy and the kid in the act. You might suggest a room change for the kid and get advice from other staff members, but most of them have their hands tied as well, because theoretically you don't know anything about the inmate's condition. Officially it is simply a case of a potential illegal sexual relationship, and it's handled that way.

In the meantime, Cell Daddy is taking care of business and smirking at you, because he knows you know. It occurs hundreds, if not thousands of times a day in this country. What's going to happen happens, and there's little you can do about it.

Conclusion: Costs

"*T*hat lying bitch killed her kids."

The thought popped into my mind the first time I saw Susan Smith on camera, spewing deception across the country. Supposedly some guy carjacked her minivan and kidnapped her two small children strapped in the back. I marveled that the media vultures didn't catch on, but I realized the cops knew she was guilty from what they didn't say and the expressions they tried to conceal.

When you work long enough with criminals, you just know.

Sometimes it happens just walking past strangers in public. Working in the Corrections field throws a dark cast on much of what we see.

Take a walk down the mall with me. I see an attractive couple window shopping. I know that smiling, attentive, good-looking guy is bad, but I can't warn his charming, naïve companion. I know by the expressions of a woman in a bookshop that she's being devious, but I can't warn that nice elderly gentleman she's preying upon. As I go past a toy store, I worry about that vulnerable child I see talking to the man who looks around and doesn't smile when he notices my scrutiny. He's got mannerisms I'm familiar with, having seen it often in prison.

Many who work in Corrections experience this. We know or strongly suspect what someone is about to do, and we can accurately predict what someone has done in the past. But if what we anticipate will happen is not happening now, and it might not happen for many hours or even weeks or months, then there's no evidence, no crime, and therefore no action to take other then watch within reason, force it from our minds when it's out of sight, hope it doesn't happen, and realize justice in life isn't assured.

The reality of working in Corrections affects us in other ways. Many of us will never truly relax in public places and situations. In our day-to-day activities, we too frequently have that millisecond of hesitation before using a pay phone or eating a meal in a restaurant, having seen and heard what sick individuals do to both. We scan behind those we talk to, subconsciously covering their backs while at the same time analyzing whether they are lying to us.

Some of us drink to deaden the effects. Some grow more distant as distrust in relationships builds. Successful marriages are rare. I don't need to seek statistics when the evidence is blatantly played out before me.

There is a cost for working in Corrections. But every day, we continue to do our job behind prison walls.

Glossary of Correctional and Inmate Terms

risons exist as a distinct society, with skewed values and philosophies separate from those of the outside world. As with any closed society, it has its own language.

Misuse of certain terms can get a "fish" (a new inmate) or a "duck" (a new officer) in deep shit. Unfortunately, there isn't a handy reference available, so the language is learned through experience. Interestingly, some experienced officers and sergeants have a very limited understanding of inmate vocabulary and are, correspondingly, ineffective in determining what is really going on in their facility.

A year and a day. Generally, the minimum sentence an inmate receives to do prison time, as opposed to a shorter sentence, which equates to less desirable jail time. In jail, an inmate normally can't smoke, has less recreational activities, has to deal with more noise and crowding, has access to less personal property, and has less opportunities to work or get education.

AB. Common abbreviation for the Aryan Brotherhood.

Actionable. When an inmate or staff member perceived as a troublemaker finally commits an act significant enough that disciplinary moves can justifiably be made.

Administration. Often shortened to "Admin." A general term referring to nonuniformed staff members with pull in a facility. They are seen as people who don't "get their hands dirty," or deal with inmates directly. A definition of who exactly constitutes the Admin varies, but it is often used by officers to distinguish "them" from "us."

Administrative Segregation. Often shortened to "Ad Seg." The act of putting an inmate into solitary confinement pending an investigation or hearing or for his protection. Distinct from disciplinary segregation, or "D Seg," when an inmate is put in the hole for punishment. Also refers to the physical place where the inmate is confined ("We put him in Ad Seg today.")

All day. A life sentence.

Aryan. Unlike the anthropological term that refers to specific Caucasians, in prison Aryan refers to inmates who identify themselves as white who have a belief system that includes the need for a separation of the races and the superiority of the white race over all others.

Aryan Brotherhood. A prison-based gang of white inmates, originally united for mutual protection against other ethnic groups rather than as a racist gang, but definitely a racially oriented group today. Old AB members can be identified by tattoos of clover leafs and Celtic symbols such as knots and crosses. Less sophisticated inmates have tattoos of skulls, "SS" runes (also called lightning bolt lettering), swastikas, and daggers. Skinheads are not generally accepted by the AB, who consider them young bucks or punks.

Aryan Nation. A sophisticated organization with a violent history on the outside. Actual Aryan Nation members are not as common as skinheads or Aryan Brotherhood members, but they are more organized and retain their community ties while in prison. They are more likely to have been members of the organization prior to coming to prison.

Attitude adjustment. A decisive but unofficial act initiated by experienced officers and/or sergeants designed to send a message and correct an unruly inmate's behavior.

Banger. Variation of "gangbanger."

Banging. Gang activity, but not necessarily shooting. What gangbangers do.

Baseline. The normal behavior of an inmate, or how the inmate acts at different times to different things. May be a pattern of behavior observed over a long period. The term "normal" is used to denote normal for that offender. If an inmate *normally* colors his face with highlighters every Tuesday and makes bird calls while standing on tables, that would be his baseline. Variations from baselines are warning signs. If he stopped making bird calls, something is wrong.

Beaner. A derogatory reference to Hispanic or, more specifically, Mexican inmates.

Beating her bush. Having sex with a woman, or a woman masturbating.

Beef. The criminal charge that led to conviction and the current incarceration. "I got a murder beef."

Been down. Incarcerated for, as in "I've been down six years."

Bent. To be high on marijuana or to be under the influence of a mild narcotic.

Bid. The procedure for securing a better job or better days off through submitting a request and being selected based on a vacancy and seniority.

Big prison. A facility with a higher security rating than another. When used by experienced staff members from major facilities now working in minimum custody facilities and camps, this term implies a hint of elitism, reminding others that they've seen and done more within the prison system. Its use also refers to the realization of the different security mind-set between prisons and other less-controlled facilities. "In big prison we'd . . ."

Big yard. The commonly used recreation area where offenders have an opportunity to exercise. More frequently, it's a location where they conduct illegal transactions, arrange illegal activities, display power in numbers, and get a hint of freedom by being outside of walls but within razor tape and chain link. A facility generally has one big yard and some smaller yards.

Bikers. Generally white inmates affiliated or seeking affiliation with a motorcycle gang. For long-term incarceration, more bikers are in the federal system than the state systems. Many so-called bikers have never been on a Harley Davidson, the motorcycle of choice for real bikers.

Billies. Possibly shortened from hillbilly, a semiderogatory term referring to white male inmates and even white male officers, most frequently used by black male inmates. Similar, but not as harsh as "white trash" or "redneck."

Bitch. Various definitions, depending on context. 1. Time in prison ("a three year bitch"). "Big bitch" is a long sentence. 2. A blatant punk, someone who is used for sex in a male prison. 3. An owned lover in a female facility ("She's my bitch.") 4. A complaint about treatment or conditions.

Biter. An inmate with a history of biting staff members, not a minor consideration when taking the individual down.

Black Gangsta Disciples. A dangerous and powerful Midwest-based prison and street gang. Abbreviated as BGD.

Black Guerilla Family. Predecessors to the BGD from the 1960s and 1970s. Most of them are deceased or otherwise inactive. Abbreviated as BGF.

Black tar. Heroin in a form that appears like tar or, more aptly, chewed up licorice. It has a sweet, cloying scent. May be found stuck to the bottom of shoes in an inmate's room because it looks like something that could have been stepped in, which can provide an argument if the inmate is caught. ("Hey man, I didn't even know I stepped in it. This prison's got so much junk in the walls that we got it on the floors and everything.")

Blanket party. A military term used by some staff explaining that an inmate was jumped by other inmates because he violated some part of the Convict Code or did something stupid that resulted in a crackdown on the entire prison population.

Blind eye. When "turning a blind eye" toward something, a staff member is pretending not to see a violation, generally minor, because he or she either supports the inmate's action, is too lazy or frightened do anything about it, or doesn't care.

Blood. A Blood belongs to the Bloods, a street gang that is generally opposed to the Crips, another street gang. Although Bloods are primarily African-American, there are Samoan, Togo Islander, and other sets and members.

Blood in, blood out. To enter a gang by a violent act or through a beating, and to leave by being a victim or taking a few shots. (See *Jumping in, Jumping out.*)

Blue Code. Borrowed from police on the outside, it is an informal code of officers that refers to backing each other up against inmates and even the Administration. Often it equates to a code of silence or turning a blind eye ("I didn't see shit"). The Blue Code is often situational and does not apply to the utterly inept or individuals who've received repeated warnings but continue to screw up.

Body alarm. A panic button on an officer's radio that summons help instantly.

Bone crusher. A very large impact or stabbing weapon.

Bones. Dominos.

Bones, made his. An inmate who has "made his bones" has achieved status through a killing.

Books. An inmate's money accounts. An inmate might have an account he can access indirectly to purchase store items, pay for postage, send money to family, and cover other expenses, and he might have another that he can't access that's for savings.

Booth officer. Working in an enclosed area, a booth officer controls the movement of the inmates in a unit or units through control of the sliders, or internal gates.

Boss. A semirespectful term for a correctional officer used by some inmates from the South. It might also be B-O-S for "son of a bitch" reversed, or simply short for crew boss.

Box. 1. A vagina. A side comment made by a con to a male officer regarding an attractive female staff member might be, "So, you been getting in that box?" which the inmate believes is a clever statement. A derogatory comment might be, "She's so used up, she ain't got no pussy, just the box it came in." 2. A boom box, or tape player/radio. 3. A carton of cigarettes. This term never refers to sparring, or to box.

Brass A military term used by some staff members to refer to the lieutenant or above, or the equivalent noncustody rank or above, including program managers, associates, deputy wardens, etc.

Breakfast. Any form of legal speed, including coffee and a cigarette, Diet Coke or Diet Pepsi, Sobe, and ephedrine, Yellow Jackets, and megavitamins.

Brother/Bro. Not limited to African-Americans, the terms brother and bro are used by Native Americans and Aryans as well as regular inmates and especially by Cons when referring to friends. Sometimes cons will refer to bros in a manner that indicates a closer (but not sexual) tie than with real relatives.

Buck up. To talk back in an overly assertive manner in response to an order from a staff member.

Bull. A correctional officer from the old school or a rougher system who relys on intimidation and physical force.

Bull dyke. A very masculine lesbian. Butch bull dyke is the apex as far as the masculine type lesbians go.

Bullet. A short sentence in prison, generally a year and a day.

Bunk buddies. Inmates who have a homosexual relationship.

Bus therapy. A claim that an inmate is being transferred repeatedly as a form of harassment to prevent visitors, mail, and personal property from catching up to him. Despite their claims, this is not an actual management tool for offenders.

Bust a cap. To shoot someone or shoot at him.

Cadillac. A filtered, factory-made cigarette.

Call out. A list that explains when and where each inmate is due at a specific work, medical, or other appointment or assignment. A very important document that some staff members can't even read but inmates are expected to understand.

Calling someone out. To challenge to a fight. Seldom used.

Camp. A minimum security facility where the inmates receive better food and better pay but still work hard.

Catcher. A receiver of a sexual act, often not voluntary, as opposed to being a pitcher.

Caught death. To catch Acquired Immune Deficiency Syndrome (AIDS).

Cell extraction. To forcibly remove an inmate from a cell by a trained team.

Cell tag. When all the inmates in an area are written up because of contraband or joint behavior, a collective punishment, often unfair. If the perpetrator is a con, he might come forward and admit guilt, but inmates are more likely to fall together, pressure a weak offender to admit guilt, or take the hit.

Cell warrior. An offender in the hole who acts up by screaming, banging, and threatening but becomes meek when the response team arrives to take him down.

Cellie. A roommate.

Chain. A group of inmates either inbound or outgoing from a facility.

Check in. To seek protective custody or otherwise be sent to segregation. A check-in may result from a direct request by an inmate or from an incident, such as hitting another inmate or threatening staff members to save face. In one unit, the common method of checking in was for an inmate to grab a slightly built sex offender and hit him once in the face in front of staff members, then immediately turn and allow himself to be cuffed up. See *seg.*

Check yourself. A warning from one inmate to another to correct behavior because a staff member is observing or in the area. Seldom heard by staff because it is whispered or said in low tones.

Cheese dick. Someone who is weak willed.

Cheese eater. A suck-up or brown noser.

Chester. A child molester.

Chicken. A semi-derogatory term describing females of sexual value or desirability.

Child mo. A child molester.

Cholo. A male Hispanic gang member.

Chronos. Chronological records of an inmate's behavior. It is a permanent part of his file.

Chuco. A Spanish term, the Hispanic equivalent of an Original Gangsta (OG).

Clique. A tight group of friends, self-labeled in a bid to avoid being called a gang. "Hanging with my clique." Sometimes called a "set."

CO. A correctional officer, or a Corrections officer.

Common area search. A routine search of areas where several inmates have access. Contraband found in these areas can seldom be pinned to any specific inmate disciplinarily. Because individual rooms are usually searched during the day and swing shifts, inmates often hide their contraband in common areas during those periods, knowing the focus of the searches and the fact that the officers on those shifts won't have much time to hit the common areas as well. Because the graveyard shift will seldom pull sleeping inmates out of their rooms for searches, the contraband goes back in the cells at night.

Complacency. A harsh accusation, but too often a realistic one, against staff members who become slack during lulls in inmate activity. Given the sometimes tedious nature of Corrections work, complacency can be difficult to combat, and a bad sergeant can create a complacent environment.

Compromise/compromised. A filthy word to correctional professionals, to be compromised is to have been duped or to give in to inmates and be used. If an officer is compromised, he or she is dirty and unredeemable in most contexts.

Con. Short for convict, a con is an inmate who knows the score and receives a modicum of deserved respect. Cons are inmates with some self-esteem and pride who usually follow the Convict Code. All cons are inmates, but not all inmates are cons.

Connected. When a con has a point of contact in the administration or custody side of the facility that he can use to get things done. Working in Corrections involves enduring a steady prescription of bitter pills, and we take them by the handful, but the one capsule that hangs in the throat involves dealing with connected cons. As officers become sergeants, sergeants become lieutenants, and on up the chain of command, they establish relationships with and remember certain inmates, sometimes over the course of twenty years. In some cases, the con has a better line of communications and perceived credibility with senior staff than a new staff member, and his opinion is more readily accepted. Cons know this and are smug about it. It's very disturbing and something you don't forget for years, even after you start doing it.

Contraband. Illicit or excess materials found during a search. Items can range from out-of-date newspapers and magazines to guns and knives.

Control. A glass booth that is like an air traffic control center for prisons, it manages the communications and movement of offenders. Hopefully manned by sharp officers and sergeants, the Control Center directs and monitors the activities of the prison.

Convict Code. An unwritten behavior code for inmates that supports the majority of cons in their objective of "doing your own time" and not snitching as well as being man enough to accept responsibility for one's actions when caught. It allows inmates to more efficiently do their nefarious acts without bringing down heat. The Cons figure that as long as things stay concealed, most of the staff will remain happy. The Convict Code is dying out as the number of cons diminish and the number of young punks who can't do their own time increases. In some ways it is disturbingly like the Blue Code, but it's individually oriented as opposed to team focused.

Cops. Some inmates use this as a generic term for any badge wearer who enforces rules, ignorantly lumping security guards, correctional officers, and law-enforcement personnel in the same category. More experienced cons generally don't use this term, as they are keenly aware of the different roles and limitations of security, corrections, and police.

Count. The physical process of individually ensuring that each offender is present. This is the most important task of custody staff and one that requires the stopping of almost all inmate activity and movement. Until it's determined that count is cleared and all offenders are accounted for, nothing else in the facility is supposed to take place.

Count is cleared. An announcement that all inmates are accounted for and regular activities can resume.

Country Club. Refers to any federal correctional facility that doesn't treat offenders like offenders. For example, one federal correctional camp actually had a golf course with check-out golf clubs for the inmates.

Crab. A derogatory term for a Crip.

Crabs. Public lice, the vermin infesting mostly the crotch area of some inmates. Crabs look like tiny flakes of skin with dark, crimson centers.

Credibility. The most important trait that can be possessed by a correctional professional as viewed by his or her peers, supervisors, and inmates. Credibility is currency, and people without it will continually question and attempt to undermine yours.

Crew. A specific, identifiable group of inmates usually selected by the staff for a function. Informally, a group of inmates who are friends and have a strong shared identity and are mutually supportive but don't act like a gang.

Crew boss. Normally a con who directs other inmates. Sometimes a staff member who supervises a specific group of inmates on a regular basis and has a working relationship established with them.

Crime partner. An individual involved in and sentenced for the same specific incident or incidents as another inmate.

Crips. One of the largest street gangs, it includes blacks, whites, Asians, and Hispanics. Originating in Los Angeles, today the gang is spread over much of the country and is very loosely organized. Crips once favored the colors blue and green (for money) and disdained red, which was associated with their rival gang, the Bloods.

Cuffs, cuffing. An informal term for handcuffs or their use.

Cut buddy. An inmate who is given a share of a score by another offender who actually made the score, even if the first man didn't participate or take a risk.

Cut loose. To sever ties with the outside or a group inside prison. An inmate cutting loose may want to do time without pressures. He also may be cut loose from his homeboys for hanging with the wrong clique.

Cutter. An inmate who scars and mutilates him or herself repeatedly. Although generally not a serous suicidal threat, a cutter has extreme mental health issues. Cutters can do horrible damage to themselves; an extreme case might even cut off his penis or her clitoris.

Cuz. Gang member, generally black. "Yo, cuz!" from someone who isn't a friend can be taken as threat as opposed to a greeting.

CYA. Cover your ass.

D seg. Disciplinary segregation.

Dancing. Fighting. Not frequently used.

Dawg. A variation of calling a man a dog, but it's an affectionate term, similar to bud. A dawg is a regular guy with regular interests, like women.

Dayroom. This is considered a common area, like a living room for a prison living unit, where the offenders meet and interact.

De-escalation. To reduce tension or to calm an upset inmate, group of inmates, or situation through the proper use of presence and verbal skills. An essential function of correctional officers.

Dick Tracying it. When an officer is pursuing an investigation doggedly that another staff member sees as worthless or not worth pursuing.

Different day, same old shit. A common exchange between an old con and an established officer, the rough equivalent of good morning, good afternoon, or good night.

Dime bag. 1/8th of an ounce, normally of marijuana.

Ding. A derogatory term for a mentally ill offender (MIO). "Nutter" in England and parts of Canada.

Dinosaur. A ponderous, "eight and a gate" officer who is deliberately slow to respond and expends the minimum effort to do his job. Dinosaur officers are generally complacent.

Dirty dicking. A petty and nasty form of "git back" where a male rubs his penis against the brim of a coffee mug, an unused envelope flap, or anywhere the target might put his or her mouth.

Dis, dissing. To show disrespect.

Disruptive behavior. A blanket term to describe inmate misbehavior, or a specific accusation when an inmate causes an incident in the vicinity of other inmates who may be influenced by it.

Disruptive group. Official terminology for a gang.

Disturbance. In the understated manner of correctional professionals, a disturbance may range from a few minutes of disruption to a full-blown riot.

Do rag. Generally worn by blacks and some Asian offenders, a do rag is a piece of cloth, most often black, worn so it completely covers the hair. It is drawn tightly across the front, back, top, and sides of the head, with some material hanging in the back. It has an intimidating appearance on already intimidating looking inmates; it's comical and pathetic on most others. If you watched the TV show "Oz" or remember the sinister, all-black-garbed street fighter in the movie *Blackhawk Down*, you've seen a do rag.

Doin' your own time. Serving the sentence while staying out of trouble and without bothering anyone else.

Drop a dime on someone. To snitch on someone. Refers to the old cost of making a phone call.

Dry cell. A cell without a bathroom and sink.

Dry snitching. 1. To inform on someone indirectly by talking aloud with the intention of being overheard by staff members, or doing obvious acts when an officer is around to attract attention. 2. To provide useless and distracting information to a staff member. 3. To brazenly inform on another inmate.

Duck. A derogatory term for a new officer.

Dump. An unofficial term for placing an inmate in segregation.

Eight and a gate. Refers to doing an eight-hour shift as a correctional officer with as little effort as possible, then departing as soon as allowed. It exemplifies a work attitude of just doing time and not getting heavily involved in what is going on in the facility. May be a single-day approach or a career aspiration.

Elder. A senior Indian (Native American) religious leader.

Fell. To get arrested and sent to prison. "The first time I fell, I was just sixteen."

Finger, fingering. To point out the guilty party.

Fish. An inmate new to being in prison. Seldom used, almost archaic.

Fixated inmate. An inmate who derives a feeling of freedom or distraction through obsessive behavior such as perpetual cleaning, floor buffing, or study of something insignificant. He may or may not seek recognition and satisfaction from the act, or he may be so caught up in his activity that everything else is incidental.

Flagged. Identified as, or selected.

Flashing gang signs. Using hand signals to communicate gang affiliation.

Float officer. To save on personnel costs, some facilities have officers who drift between living units. They are suppose to spend equal time in each one, but the reality is they often go see their buddies or linger where the pretty officer works or where the better coffee can be found.

Foglines. When visibility is diminished due to fog, staff members are placed along the perimeters and inmate movement is restricted. The assignment is always cold, it's generally for a long time, and it's a bitch.

Four pointed. When an offender must be strapped down for his or her protection or for the protection of other staff and offenders.

Freeworld. The outside of the prison.

Friendliness. A flaw that will be exploited by the inmates; seen as a weakness by staff.

Fronting. To confront someone or to point out an error made by another in front of others.

Front Street. To put someone on Front Street is to expose him to everyone, in a major manner, such as confronting him in front of the whole shift.

Fudge packer. An inmate who is the penetrator during anal sex.

Gang. A group of inmates who are affiliated for criminal activities. Officially referred to as a "threat security group," "disruptive group," or other PC title in some facilities.

Gangbanger. A member of a gang, generally young, who is less mature, more vocal, and generally still out to make a name for him or herself through affiliation with a recognized gang. May or may not have been jumped in to a gang.

Gangsta, gangster. An established gang member with credentials, including the commission of crimes and the backing of others. Higher than a gangbanger but not up to being an Original Gangsta.

Gat. A gun used by inmates who are wannabes and desperately want to be seen as gangstas.

Gate money. A paltry sum given to departing inmates who don't have money on the books. This $40 to $100 is often all they have with which to restart their lives. It is considered enough money to get them away from the vicinity of the prison.

Getting short. When an inmate is nearing the end of his time in prison. The inmate might become very careful if he wants to get out, or he may become reckless if he doesn't want to get out.

Git back. A "get back," or something done for revenge.

Goon squad. An unofficial term for the response and backup staff members.

Gooning. To use force on an inmate by the goon squad.

Gray Bar Hotel. A geeky term for prison.

Gun. Generally refers to a tattoo gun rather than a firearm.

Guns. Muscular arms and/or pectoral muscles.

Hard time. Indicates that the inmate either doesn't know how to do time, or is having a rough time making the adjustment, or is so bothered by inside and outside factors that he's not making it. Unofficial staff variations of "hard time" can mean being shaken down, beaten, or raped, or simply being in an unpleasant facility with a rough schedule.

Heart, having heart. Indicates an inmate who is strong and holds to his convictions.

Hit. An attack; a planned, violent act, generally inmate on inmate but may be on a staff member. A hit isn't necessarily done to kill.

Hit the bricks. A verbal order to walk away. The equivalent of "beat it" or "get lost."

Hit the streets. To be released from prison, but with a connotation that the individual is going to hit the ground running and make up lost time through a lot of activity. This may be good, like getting a job, seeing the children, and making up with the woman, or bad, like enjoying the thug life maxed out, doing a payback, taking a lot of drugs, or just going back to what he was doing before he got busted.

Hittin' it. A statement or question regarding sex with a female. An inmate may ask an officer, "That new CO with them big brown eyes and all that hair—you been hittin' it?" The term can also refer to an activity as innocuous as studying hard.

Ho. A derogatory term used by many inmates to refer to women.

Holding. To carry or conceal, with some risk, something for someone else, often drugs.

Holding court. When some inmate groups settle differences semiformally and covertly because they don't want staff involvement. Black Islamic inmates occasionally use this technique when a member is showing problems with the faith or making them look bad.

Holding court in the streets. [Inmates] Settling things man to man without legal involvement. For example, a father who kills a man who molested his daughter held court in the streets.

Hole. The politically incorrect term for segregation.

Homeboy, homie, homes. Someone from the same gang, neighborhood, or ethnic group.

Hook. What an inmate uses to trap and compromise a staff member.

Hooked up. Set up in a positive manner. "With that sweet volunteer eyeballing me, I was all hooked up."

Horse. Street name for heroin.

House. A cell or a room to which an inmate is assigned. Use of this term denotes ownership.

Hug-a-thug. A derogatory term used by some correctional staff members for any program or "treatment" effort to make the lives of inmates easier. Frequently used to show others that the speaker is hard-core and experienced.

Hustle. The sanctioned or unsanctioned "job," or source of income, for inmates while in prison. Payment is often in the form of "store" (i.e., items from another inmate's canteen supplies) or money. May include legal work for other inmates, beadwork, tattooing, drawing, writing letters, etc. Some hustles are allowed; some are not.

Ice. Crystal methamphetamine.

IMU. Intensive Management Unit, better known as the hole, or segregation. In some systems, Special Management Unit.

Incident. In the sometimes understated and vague jargon of Corrections, an incident is an event that can range from a heated verbal exchange with an inmate that requires follow-up to an out-and-out riot or situation resulting in a death.

Industries, prison industries. Most prison systems engage inmates in some form of work, usually agricultural. In some cases they perform subcontracting for real manufacturers, construct furniture for state agencies, or, more familiar to most readers, make license plates.

Infraction. Sometimes known as a disciplinary report (DR), an infraction is a violation of the rules that is documented through a report and requires a hearing or a determination of guilt, followed by a sanction if warrented. An infraction can be a minor one, called a general infraction, or a serious one, which can impact the inmate in a greater way.

Infraction, ganging. To "gang infractions," several staff members write infractions on the same inmate for the same incident in an attempt to ensure the inmate receives severe sanctions for his or her behavior. Ganging infractions is generally considered wrong.

Infraction, stacking. To "stack infractions," a staff member writes several infractions for the same incident so the inmate will receive different hearings and separate sanctions for a series of misbehaviors that occurred during roughly the same period or are somehow linked, hoping the inmates receives several sanctions (e.g., several hours of extra duty, room restriction, etc.) instead of one sanction from one guilty finding. Devious staff members will wait a day and submit an infraction to a different sergeant, not mentioning that the incident has already been infracted. Often seen as a transparent attempt to manipulate the system and, more importantly, the sergeant.

Inmate. Either a generic term for any felon in the population of a facility, or a derogatory term for prisoners who don't know how to do time.

Institutional memory. A source for unwritten sets of procedures and codes stemming from things that have happened in the past. Often determines why something is or isn't done.

Institutionalized. When an inmate has been down for such a long time that he's unable or unwilling to face adaptation to living outside or is too well-adjusted to life within the system. The librarian in the movie *Shawshank Redemption* who commits suicide after being released is a good portrayal of an institutionalized inmate. Sometimes institutionalized inmates commit a new crime so they can be sent back to prison more rapidly.

Intern. A college-level student engaged in a training program geared toward giving him or her experience in Corrections. Generally, interns are underpaid and underfoot. Some are outstanding and enthusiastic; others need help tying their shoes. Guess which ones seem to get hired faster.

Isolate and contain. During a response to an incident, a procedure that separates involved inmates from each other and uninvolved inmates, enabling the site to be controlled as soon as possible.

Jack, jacked. From "hijack," to rob with the threat or use of violence.

Jacked up. To correct a misbehaving inmate decisively and aggressively through the use of verbal skills. Sometimes, jacking up an inmate might involve subtle hints of a willingness to use defensive tactics. Usually, it's a stern reminder that the inmate is being noticed and will be dealt with officially if he or she continues the behavior. Staff members sometimes jack up each other when they feel such a confrontation is merited.

Jacket. An inmate's reputation, always negative. Most commonly heard as a "snitch' jacket."

Jail. City or county correctional facilities (prisons belong to the state and federal governments). A prison sentence is generally comprised of "a year and a day" or more, while sentences of a year or under merit jail time. Inmates sometimes ask for a year and a day over a shorter sentence, even months shorter, because conditions in jails are often appalling due to overcrowding and lack of programming or, more importantly, lack of personal property and cigarettes.

Jailer. A county or city correctional officer.

Jailhouse lawyer. A con or inmate who believes he knows the laws through years of studying in the facility's law library and who continually attempts to file appeals or lawsuits to benefit himself or other inmates. Some are effective; most are clowns who waste staff time.

Joint. The prison facility, or a marijuana cigarette (not frequently used).

Joto. A derogatory Spanish term for homosexual.

Juice. Real power, or the ability to influence. "He has juice."

Jump. To initiate a fight.

Jumpin' in. To endure a right of initiation into a street gang. Usually involves getting one's butt kicked by members of the gang, but instead can be a requirement to commit an illegal act, up to and including a hit.

Jumpin' out. Getting one's butt kicked on the way out of the gang as a penalty for leaving the ranks. Often, jumpin' out is intended to be a severe enough penalty to discourage individuals from leaving the gang.

Keister. To secrete contraband up one's rectum to avoid confiscation by staff. Periodically, X-rays of guns and knives keistered by some unidentified inmate make the rounds.

Key control. The strict procedures for issuing and handling keys required by a correctional facility.

Kick rocks. To leave; beat it. "Go kick rocks."

Kicked to the curb. To be ignored or rejected callously or harshly.

Kite. A written request, usually on an appropriate form, from an inmate to a staff member requesting some action.

Knuckle dragger. Also known as "goon." Used by modern correctional professionals when referring to the old-style of prison guard who relied more on muscles than brains and slamming, cuffing, and stuffing than verbal deescalation. Although considered an outmoded method of conducting business, knuckle draggers are still around and are still necessary.

Lay-in. An excused absence from work for a medical or other reason.

Leg off. A mythical repellant for inmate and staff brown nosers. It might even exist, since many officers have bottles labeled "Leg Off" on their desks to deal with inmates.

Leg rider. A suck-up or brown noser.

Let it go. To get past an irritation or problem; to drop it. Frequently, new officers let an inmate piss them off and they don't drop the matter. More than casual advice at times, "Let it go" is a warning that the officer may not be acting professionally and will be causing more problems than solving them.

Lifer. An inmate doing a life sentence.

Lip. A defense attorney, generally paid for, as opposed to a public defender.

Lipstick lesbian. A female inmate, either attractive in a conventional sense or at least very feminine, who engages in homosexuality.

Lock down. When the inmates are confined to their rooms or cells in response to an incident. Often indicates that a very significant security threat has been realized and is being responded to. Normally not a punishment, although inmates view a lock down as a collective punishment.

Lock psychosis. A mind-set developed by many officers and staff members, sometimes close to an obsession, where everything should be secured (locked) and checked repeatedly. When an officer checks his car door immediately after stepping out, then walks back on a regular basis to check again, he's got lock psychosis.

LT. Common abbreviated term for a lieutenant. A correctional lieutenant, unlike military ones, is an experienced staff member who served time as a sergeant and demonstrated correctional understanding and a willingness to take charge. Conversely, he can be a cheese eating back stabber who caught the attention of the Admin while serving as a sergeant. Most LTs know how the system works better than the sergeants.

Macking. Efforts by an inmate to make headway in getting what he wants from a woman or girl, including talking, grinning, laughing, cajoling, and even intimidating. A would-be play, without the sophistication.

Mack Daddy. An image that an inmate wishes to project that he can influence and control the woman around him, and/or he believes he is successful at manipulating younger women. Mack Daddy's generally are larger black males in their late thirties or older.

Made. Has been identified, but in a bad way. One time an inmate came up to me and said he had to PC. He'd been telling inmates he was involved in regular crimes such as robbery and dealing, but a TV show revealed his true crimes and the fact that he was a snitch. He said, "I've been made."

Mainline. The dining facility, or the period during which the inmates go to the dining facility to eat. Also relates to IV drug use, as in "mainlining some smack," a colorful reference to heroin use.

Man, the. "The Man" is generally an authority figure in an official capacity, as opposed to parents or teachers.

Man down. A call for assistance. More specifically, notification that help is needed and medical staff needs to respond or get ready. A man down call can be for an officer or inmate, but generally it is used for inmates. "Officer down" is considered much more significant.

Marked. To be labeled negatively. "He marked me as a snitch." Can indicate that time is running out.

Meds. Medication.

Meth. Methamphetamines.

Milkshake. A combination of urine and feces shaken in a container and thrown on unsuspecting staff members by inmates.

MIO. Mentally Ill Offender.

Mud. Coffee.

Mule. A weaker inmate used by another to smuggle or hold drugs and other contraband.

Mystery date. Due to high staff turnover, it's possible for an officer not to have a regular partner, and it's luck of the draw on who he'll be working with. As with social mystery dates, it can go well or terribly.

Nada. Spanish for nothing.

Naïve. To be trusting because of inexperience and lack of exposure to the real world. While charming on the outside, this is the worst state to be in while in a correctional environment.

New hire. Any officer still learning the job, including transfers unfamiliar with the facility.

No lie. What an inmate says when he is trying to be truthful, with emphasis.

Noreno. A prison gang member from Northern California. Uses the number 14 as an identifier. Seen by their rivals, the more urbane Surenos, as less sophisticated migrant farm workers.

Nothing coming. Indicates nothing will be done for the inmate beyond what's required because the inmate has violated some value or rule that can't be overlooked or has otherwise burned his or her bridges.

Offender. A politically correct term for inmates or incarcerated prisoners.

Officer. The appropriate term for a uniformed correctional professional below the rank of sergeant (or corporal, if in that system). Today's officers are trained in Corrections in a manner that relies less on force and intimidation and more on verbal skills, observation, and documentation. "Prison guard" is an obsolete and inaccurate term.

Original Gangsta. Abbreviated as OG, a gang member from the old crew, a "real deal" gangbanger.

Old school. Used by both inmates and staff members, "the old school" refers to the way it never really was but was close to being—rougher, more direct, and with more violence-related options. Use of the term indicates the speaker has a depth of experience.

On the rag. Abbreviated as OTR, used to describe a female staff member who the inmates feel is coming down too hard on them while enforcing policy and not accepting any crap.

Operator. A con who knows how to successfully wheel and deal and work the system.

Orientation. A series of briefings during which newly arriving staff and inmates are shown the ropes and taught how to work within the system. Staff and inmate orientations are, of course, separate.

Oscars. The author's term for crabby staff members who revel in the belief that everyone else is wrong and disagree with commonly held beliefs and understandings out of habit.

Out, an. An acceptable excuse or waiver. Sometimes giving an inmate an out, or a way of getting free of a jam, can resolve an issue quickly.

Out of pocket. Uncalled for; something that shouldn't be suggested or asked. "Hey, that comment was out of pocket; you got no right saying that."

Ownership. Giving staff members or inmates a say in developing a policy or procedure so they can't justifiably bitch about it later on. Also, to get input from staff or inmates to ensure that the best practice is emplaced.

Packing. To be carrying contraband on (or in) one's person.

Painter. An inmate with a mental illness who decorates the walls of his cell, and usually himself, with feces. Unfortunately, not an uncommon behavior. Also called a cell painter and a Picasso.

Papa. A female inmate who is masculine and sexually aggressive and takes a dominant role in a homosexual relationship and running other business.

Paper bullets. From the military, documents that can detrimentally affect inmates, such as memorandums, observation reports, and witness statements. A paper bullet may be aimed at staff or inmates. For inmates, it can affect custody level; for staff, careers.

Papers. Sentencing documents received from courts that are proof of the inmate's offense. An inmate may demand to see another inmate's papers, which is a suggestion that he believes the other to be a sex offender or possibly a snitch. Smart inmates keep their papers ready but become angry when asked to show them. Cons don't have to show anyone their papers.

Peckerwood. A distinct term, refering to white male offenders who emphasize a "hick" attitude. Although generally racist, it is not their focus, and they get along with other offenders better than the skinheads. In appearance, think of Axel Rose of the rock group Guns 'n Roses. A female version is a featherwood.

Pica. Spanish for a shank or a knife.

Pile. The weight pile.

Pill line. Where and when medications are distributed.

Pillow biter. An involuntary punk.

Pin joint, pinner. Slender marijuana cigarettes common in prison. About the diameter of a lollipop stick.

Pinging. When a mentally ill offender "goes off," or is acting up or otherwise winding up toward an episode. "C Unit's got a body alarm, and we got a ding pinging in F Unit."

Piss test. Urinalysis, or UA, a test for illicit substance abuse.

Pitcher. The sexually aggressive offender, as opposed to the catcher.

Player, playa. An individual who thinks he can successfully manipulate the system or, more frequently, women to his own ends.

Playing. Skillfully manipulating someone else or the system.

PO. Probation Officer.

Popped. Caught doing something; busted.

Porter. An inmate used as a janitor.

Potty watch. Also called "shit watch." A special watch that takes place when staff suspects that an inmate has ingested a balloon full of illicit substances. The inmate is placed in a dry cell in a special garment that prevents him from accessing fecal waste if he voids while wearing it.

Power walk. Several inmates belonging to one group walking abreast in the big yard as a show of solidarity and strength to both inmates and staff. Strutting, grins or hard expressions, and aggressive posturing accompanies a power walk.

Practices. Practices generally do not have a relationship with policy, but they are how we get things done or are supposed to get things done. There are three types:

- Accepted practice—The allowed, preferred, or accepted method of dealing with anything. This term comes up instantly when a practice is questioned, or when questioning a peer on his or her judgment.
- Best practice—What management would like to establish as the standard and/or the means of accomplishing things, even though they can't enforce it. Seldom is the best practice the actual practice, and no one practices the best practice on a regular basis because it is often seen as the ideal of someone who is out of touch with the reality of Corrections.
- Past practice—How things were allegedly done in the past. A citation of past practice is akin to an excuse or explanation for a practice that is currently being called into question.

Precisely vague. A nebulous response that doesn't exactly answer the question but is exactly what you'll say when someone asks you something because it fits so well.

Presence. A simple procedure used by staff members to control inmate behavior. By simply walking through an area and being seen (having presence), they can keep things quieter and cut down on illegal activities. Presence can include having video cameras, armed tower guards, and several goons standing by.

Priors. Prior convictions that influenced the sentencing of an inmate's current stint.

Programming. Following the classes and work schedule designed by a counselor to best rehabilitate an inmate.

Progressive discipline. Increasing the level of punishment as a disruptive behavior continues.

Protective custody. Abbreviated as PC, a status sought by or given to inmates thought to be in danger from other inmates. Involves isolation.

Pruno. An alcoholic drink made from starch, yeast, fruit, and often sugar and heat. Sometimes called "raisin jack" or "jungle juice" in other systems.

Public pretender. What inmates call court-appointed lawyers, properly known as public defenders.

Pull. The ability to get something done through influence, usually with a small amount of effort.

Pumping out viruses, pumping out the virus. A sexually active, dominant inmate transmitting AIDS.

Punk. An inmate on the receiving end of homosexual acts, or the act itself. Calling an inmate a punk can lead to a fight.

Quick Reaction Team. The first response or back-up in a prison. Generally it consists of a shift sergeant, or designated sergeant, and several response and movement officers. Abbreviated as QRT.

Rabbit. To run.

Rape-O. An inmate with a sex offense, usually against an adult rather than a child.

Rat. The act of or being a snitch.

Really bad situation. Anything involving a potential or actual incident of violence and injury or death.

Reals. Any brand name item, especially cigarettes, as opposed to store brand or generic.

Response & Movement Officer. R&Ms are officers assigned to zones rather than locations. They are the first ones to respond to a situation after the officers in the immediate area. They are a "security" post rather than a program or unit post. Formerly and unofficially called the "goon squad."

Riding the leg. Becoming overly friendly with staff in order to seek favors.

Rig. Syringe, often improvised, to inject heroin. A "fully loaded rig" is ready to go. Also a term for a tattoo gun (uncommon).

Righteous. An archaic term meaning good, right on, more than meets the standards. "That 4th of July BBQ was righteous."

Ritualized behavior. When an inmate or a staff member adopts and maintains a pattern of activity, generally making something mundane into something significant, such as putting on one's coat and gloves or making a cup of coffee. Sometimes it's a subconscious means of performing the equivalent of a superstitious gesture. The person can derive anxiety from not being permitted to complete the ritual because they see it as somehow ensuring their safety. It is an odd defense mechanism.

Rock solid. As reliable as can be hoped for.

Roll up, rolled up. To pack up an inmate's belongings because he is going to be transported to segregation, or to send that inmate to segregation. This old term comes from the practice of rolling up an inmate's blankets and mattresses when his room was vacated.

Run it down. To trace a rumor or story to its point of origin, or to fill others in on the details.

Running interference. When an inmate distracts staff members to provide cover for other inmates engaged in illegal activities. The most common technique is to ask questions of and joke around with staff members.

Sally port. An area where movement is controlled by two consecutive sliding doors, with only one open at a time to maintain security.

School yard rules. An expectation for male behavior, taught to them from a very young age.

Examples: Bullies exist, and dealing with bullying is part of the jumping-in process. Males are supposed to stand up for themselves and show backbone, yet some of the dogging is good-natured or just part of doing business, so an under or overreaction can cause problems for new officers.

Schooled. Taught as to how it should be.

Score. An unauthorized gain of material of any kind, through direct theft or some other crafty activity. It has more than intrinsic value, just as a fisherman's catch might taste better than a store-bought fish.

Scrap. An inmate who will dig cigarette butts out of an ashtray to salvage bits of tobacco or who will beg for items from other inmates. Uncommon.

Screw. An archaic and possibly suspect term popularized by Hollywood in the 1930s to refer to prison guards by cons. If anyone uses the term to describe an officer, they are either joking or have watched too many movies.

Security threat group. The proper, politically correct term for a gang. Abbreviated as STG.

Seg. Segregation, the hole. There are three different types of segregation: ad seg, or administrative segregation, D seg, or disciplinary segregation, and IMU, or intensive management unit segregation. Ad seg includes protective custody, time pending a hearing, and time pending an investigation and is not considered a punishment. Disciplinary segregation is given after a hearing and a sanction has been issued. IMU is for the animals unfit to be housed even with other inmates.

Senior staff member. Anyone with many years of experience in Corrections, or the person with more time in uniform. This individual may be held more responsible than his or her peers because of his or her level of experience and the expectations that allows.

Seniority. A status gained by staff members through longevity of employment, which may lead to benefits such as not being picked for mandatory overtimes or being given preference for good jobs.

Set. A gang, the people an offender hangs with and is tight with. Almost never refers to Caucasian offenders except for wannabes.

Shake down. To search an individual or location thoroughly.

Shamming. When a person isn't doing what he's supposed to be doing, or doing just enough that it gives the appearance of work being done.

Shank. An improvised knife. May be made of plastic or metal, but traditionally from the spring steel shank of a prison-issue shoe, sharpened into a useful form. A true shank is a very decent find during a search.

Shermed. High on PCP. Also, the effects of smoking a regular cigarette that's been soaked in formaldehyde.

Shiv. An archaic term for a shank. Seldom used in Corrections these days, but occasionally used in the East.

Shooting up. Injecting heroin or other drugs intravenously.

Shop steward. In a prison with a union, an officer or sergeant who represents staff members in trouble or who are having a disagreement with management. This is an elected position, usually an additional, outside duty to employment.

Short. When an inmate doesn't have much time left in prison. For example, an inmate with "three days and a wake up" is very short.

Shot rag. A piece of cloth, usually a T-shirt or washcloth, used by a masturbating inmate to catch his semen. A really nasty discovery during a cell search.

Slammed. To be taken down forcefully by the goon squad.

Sliders. Massive metal-framed and glass sliding doors, almost always remotely controlled, used for security separation.

Smack. 1. Heroin. 2. Talking smack, which is to bullshit.

Snake pit. A new officer's view of the custody staff when he or she doesn't know who to trust and doesn't understand the system.

Snitch. An informant.

Snitch gram. An anonymous note that exposes illicit behavior of an inmate or staff member. Can be real or fictitious.

Snitching yourself off. Doing something intentionally or inadvertently that identifies an error you made. May be hidden in a memo or a report.

Special Response Team. An elite group of staff members who perform higher risk operations in a correctional environment. This all-volunteer unit receives extensive training. Abbreviated as SRT.

Sprung. To get out of incarceration.

Square. An infrequently used term for a cigarette, generally used by middle-aged or older blacks.

Stinger. A device with a coiled wire and plug used to heat water.

Store. The consumable goods purchased by an inmate from the canteen, it is the primary currency and trade commodity in prisons.

Straight. On the level.

Strawberry. A woman willing to do anything, usually sexual and nasty, for drugs, most specifically for crack cocaine.

Street name. The nickname of an inmate. Some are related to their names, such as "Kid" Curry or "Black" Jack. Others reflect a link with a name and an object ("Money" Greene), a physical attribute ("Horse"), a deficiency or flaw ("Gimpy"), or an activity or behavior ("Icer").

Streets. The outside world, from a criminal's perspective.

Strong arming. To use intimidation and sometimes actual force to get an inmate to give up store items.

Suits. A seldom-used term referring to administrative personnel.

Surenos. Mexican-American gang members from Southern California. Rivals to the Nurenos, they use the number 13.

Sweated. Being pressured for doing some act or possessing some property.

Sweet. An individual who is suspected of being gay.

Tag. Infraction.

Tat. A tattoo, or tattooing.

Three hots and a cot. Refers to three hot meals and a place to sleep, indicating that prison is a slack experience for inmates. Extended version: "Three hots and a cot and a punk in the bunk."

Throw down. To fight.

Ticket. An infraction or disciplinary report.

Tier. The walkway outside or in front of cells or rooms in a living unit.

Tort. A civil action designed to address a perceived wrong or loss through monetary compensation.

Toss. To search a cell or area in a disrespectful manner, leaving it in shambles, or to do so in a thorough manner to send a message, or to urgently search for dangerous contraband.

Turn out. To set up as a punk for business and/or to introduce someone to deviant behaviors.

Tweaking. When a meth head goes off from his addiction and a serious dose. A very dangerous time for those around him and for himself.

24/7. Twenty four hours a day, seven days a week. Continuously.

24-7 to your 8. Refers to the fact that inmates have twenty-four hours a day, seven days a week, to come up with methods to "trip up" staff members, while most officers only have eight hours a day, five days a week, on their regular schedule to counter it.

Unauthorized pets/unauthorized visitors. Casual code for an inmate who has crabs, head lice, or scabies.

Uncle. A fed, or federal official, referring to Uncle Sam. In a woman's prison, a woman who looks out for the girls, sometimes turning them out, and who watches business for a daddy.

Unit. A defined section of a facility with its own leadership, regular staff, and assigned inmates.

Unit team. Sometimes used generically to explain the involvement of the unit sergeant, counselors, and custody unit supervisor to make decisions about an inmate and/or an issue, or the process of making the decision regarding an inmate's classification. "We did a unit team on inmate Garza today."

Wacked. Nuts, or experiencing the effects of PCP.

Walking the tier. A job performed by a unit officer assigned to watch offenders in their housing units and look, listen, and even smell for illicit activity. It's like an in-house patrol. Much inmate activity is discovered and snitches are frequently encountered while walking the tier. It has some hazards because the officer is generally alone while doing it.

War path. Infrequently used, when a sergeant or officer nails inmates for everything possible.

Wargaming, An informal but valuable training technique that prepares an officer to face various situations by exposing him or her to the potential situations through discussion.

White bread. A person, generally an honest, good-natured Caucasian, who can be conned out of money. A staple for criminals.

White money. Real currency within a prison.

Wire. The route, and the individuals involved, for transferring illicit items, usually narcotics, from one inmate to another or from one point to another.

Wolf pack. A comparison of custodial staff member behaviors with lupine patterns in the wild. Not intended to be utterly unfavorable, this comparison recognizes the dynamics of a group that experiences power struggles and requires members to fulfill such roles as Alfas (leaders) Betas (secondary leaders), and Omegas (scapegoats) to survive in a threatening environment and the need for certain harsh behaviors. With a wolf pack, as with custody staff, you are either in or out.

Wolf tickets. If a person talks in a tough manner and continually challenges others, he is writing wolf tickets. This is a very negative behavior, as no one can keep it up day after day, and few can really back it.

Working somebody. To manipulate someone.

Write-up. An infraction.

Yard. An area where inmates partake in outdoor recreation or exercise.

Young Turks. New staff members who come into a facility believing they are better trained, smarter, and more aggressive then their more experienced counterparts, often spurned on by training that warned them about the complacency of their peers. Some Young Turks are perceived as know-it-alls, and they fail to listen to the advice provided by more experienced and senior officers, leading to friction and bitterness. They are the opposite of dinosaur officers.